STEALTH MARKETING

By **T.J. Rohleder**
(a.k.a. "The Blue Jeans Millionaire")

Other Great Titles from T.J. Rohleder:

Ruthless Marketing Secrets (Series)
The 2-Step Marketing Secret That Never Fails
Instant Cash Flow
The Power of Hype
3 Steps to Instant Profits
Money Machine
The Blue Jeans Millionaire
How to Turn Your Kitchen or Spare Bedroom into a Cash Machine
The Black Book of Marketing Secrets (Series)
The Ultimate Wealth-Maker
Four Magical Secrets to Building a Fabulous Fortune
The Ruthless Marketing Attack
How to Get Super Rich in the Opportunity Market
$60,000.00 in 90 Days
How to Start Your Own Million Dollar Business
Fast Track to Riches
Five Secrets That Will Triple Your Profits
Ruthless Copywriting Strategies
25 Direct Mail Success Secrets That Can Make You Rich
Ruthless Marketing
24 Simple and Easy Ways to Get Rich Quick
How to Create a Hot Selling Internet Product in One Day
50 in 50
Secrets of the Blue Jeans Millionaire
Shortcut Secrets to Creating High-Profit Products
Foolproof Secrets of Sucessful Millionaires
How to Make Millions While Sitting on Your Ass
500 Ways to Get More People to Give You More Money

FIRST EDITION

ISBN 1-933356-98-7

TABLE OF CONTENTS

Introduction:

By T.J. Rohleder

CONGRATULATIONS for buying this book! As you'll see—this is one of the smartest decisions you'll ever make! Does that sound like hype? YOU BET! And yet, it's the ABSOLUTE TRUTH!

Here's why... Inside this book, you'll discover some of my all time greatest marketing secrets for getting more people to spend more money, more often, with greater efficiency than ever before! Yes, these are some of my greatest marketing secrets for ATTRACTING and RETAINING the very best clients and customers in your market and getting them to do business with YOU, instead of all of your competitors!

Does that sound exciting to you?

IF SO—YOU'RE GOING TO LOVE THIS BOOK! You see, in today's world, having the very best product or service is NOT ENOUGH... The individuals and companies who experience the GREATEST SUCCESS in the marketplace are the ones who are the very best marketers. These are the people who truly understand all the ways to find, get, and keep MORE of the very best customers and clients. The people who know how to do this can DOMINATE THEIR MARKETPLACE and have a very real unfair advantage over all of their competition... And now...

One of these people can be YOU!

STEALTH MARKETING!

Yes, you're about to discover some of my all time greatest marketing secrets that have generated millions of dollars in sales and profits for my small company. Now, I'm THRILLED to give them to you and to offer my help, support, and guidance to enable YOU to make all the money you want and need. All the basic secrets you need are in this book and in the special FREE GIFT that I I'll tell you about in a minute.

But before I get to that, let me first tell you a bit more about the TITLE of this book. As you'll see, the first chapter of this book tells you all about Direct Mail Marketing. **I call this powerful form of marketing STEALTH MARKETING because it flies under the radar of your competition.** With all kinds of other marketing, your biggest competitors can keep tabs on you and see exactly what you're doing to build your business. But not so with Direct Mail. This is the marketing method that can let you QUIETLY DOMINATE YOUR MARKET without any of your competitors knowing what you're doing to make your money.

Direct mail marketing gives you a REAL ADVANTAGE over all of these other people because it's a private way that you can ATTRACT & RETAIN the very best clients and customers in your market. When done correctly, this gives you a major competitive advantage that you can use to find, get, and keep MORE of the very best customers and clients in your marketplace—and do it in such a way that none of your competitors know what you're up to!

I call Direct Mail Marketing "STEALTH MARKETING" because this is A VERY PRIVATE WAY to quietly dominate your market.

The more you know about Direct Mail Marketing, the more

excited you'll be! Remember, the words of Aristotle Onassis, the Greek shipping billionaire, who once said, "Success in business is to know something that your competition does not know." This 'thing they don't know' is the entire subject of marketing in general, but as in the title of this book it's Direct Mail Marketing. You see, most of the companies you compete with think that Direct Mail is simply mailing some postcards or letters. That's it. That's all they know about using Direct Mail to build their business — and as the old saying goes, "A little knowledge is a dangerous thing!" Because they never DIG DEEPER for the truth. Their small amount of knowledge keeps them from making the huge sums of money that they could and should be making with this method.

But you won't make this mistake. Just go over Chapter One and discover the truth about Direct Mail Marketing and why it can give you a major advantage over all of your biggest competitors. Let this fact excite you! Then go through the other chapters of this book an get the rest of my PROVEN MARKETING SECRETS that give you the power to find, get, and keep MORE of the very best customers and clients in your marketplace.

And to reward you for purchasing this book, I have...

A great FREE business-building gift for you!

Yes, I have a gift waiting for you that can DRAMATICALLY INCREASE YOUR SALES AND PROFITS! Here's what it's all about: I spent TEN FULL YEARS writing down all of the greatest marketing and success secrets I discovered during that time period. Each day, I took a few notes and, at the end of a decade, I had a GIANT LIST of 6,159 powerful secrets! This list is ALMOST 1,000 PAGES of hardcore money-making ideas and strategies!**

STEALTH MARKETING!

Best of all, this massive collection is now YOURS ABSOLUTELY FREE! Just go to: www.6159FreeSecrets.com and get it NOW! As you'll see, this complete collection of 6,159 of my greatest marketing and success secrets, far more valuable than those you can buy from others for $495 to $997, is absolutely **FREE.** No cost, no obligation.

Why am I giving away this GIANT COLLECTION of secrets, that took ONE DECADE to discover and compile, FOR FREE? That's simple; I believe many of the people who receive these 6,159 secrets in this huge 955 page PDF document will want to obtain some of our other books and audio programs and participate in our special COACHING PROGRAMS. However, you are NOT obligated to buy anything—now or ever.

I know you're serious about making more money or you wouldn't be reading this. So go to: www.6159FreeSecrets.com and get this complete collection of 6,159 of my greatest marketing and success secrets right now! **You'll get this GREAT FREE GIFT in the next few minutes, just for letting me add you to my Client mailing list,** and I'll stay in CLOSE TOUCH with you... and do all I can to help you make even more money with my proven marketing strategies and methods.

So with all this said, let's begin...

** WARNING: This complete collection of 6,159 marketing and success secrets contains MANY CONTROVERSIAL ideas and methods. Also, it was originally written for MY EYES ONLY and for a few VERY CLOSE FRIENDS. Therefore, the language is X-RATED in some places [I got VERY EXCITED when I wrote many of these ideas and used VERY FOUL LANGUAGE to get my ideas across!] so 'IF' you are EASILY OFFENDED or do NOT want to read anything OFFENSIVE, then please do both of us a favor and DO NOT go to my website and download this FREE gift. THANK YOU for your understanding.

CHAPTER ONE

❖ ❖ ❖

Direct Mail Marketing is really "Stealth Marketing." *You are flying under the radar!*

None of your competitors ever really know exactly what you're doing! This is a smarter way to do business.

❖ ❖ ❖

Direct Mail Marketing is Really Stealth Marketing

Back when Russ von Hoelscher first started working with us, we were bringing in about $500 a day, on average, and had been in business for about six months. Within nine months of the time we started working with Russ, our income shot up to almost $100,000 a week—over $14,000 a day. **That's more than a 28-fold increase!** Russ did a lot of things for us, but most importantly, he got us started in direct mail—and that's a uniquely powerful way to make money. **I can't stress enough how extremely lucrative it can be, and you should learn everything you can about it.**

Direct mail marketing is really stealth marketing: you're flying under the radar, by and large. **None of your competitors ever have to know exactly what you're doing. This is a smarter way to do business.** Now, some of your competitors are sneaky: they'll end up on your mailing list using false names and similar tactics. We know for a fact that we have a few of our competitors on our lists, and we can't get them off, because not only don't we know who they are, they're on our list under multiple different names—and they buy from us just to get on our list and stay on it. **But with the exception of those people (who are very few and far between, I imagine) what you're doing with direct mail is entirely opaque to your competitors.**

There are many, many things that you can do within direct

mail, and many ways to approach the marketing effort itself. **For example, you can segment your costumer list in a variety of ways. Let's say you divide it by products and services.** You may have ten different products and services by which you segment, and you'll see that you have some crossovers in your customer base: Let's say some of your costumers have bought two or three of your products, and some have bought four. A few of them have bought all ten, but you have large numbers of costumers who have bought just one. You can do things with direct mail marketing to send your offers only to the list of people who maybe bought only one or two of your products. **You can communicate with them in an entirely different way than you communicate with your rest of your clients.**

We always say that with database marketing, the left hand never has to know what the right hand is doing. Now, this sounds a little sneaky, but it's just a metaphor; the point is, **you can keep everything separate, and there's a lot of real privacy here.** You're spending a lot more money when you do that, of course. **That's the worst thing about direct mail: it's is the most expensive marketing medium possible, other than cold calling or having a sales rep going from door to door.** And yet, it's not about what something costs; you can't look at it that way. What something costs doesn't even matter: profits matter. **So with direct mail, you often spend more money to reach fewer but better qualified people; but ultimately, dollar for dollar, it's money well spent if you do it right.**

But direct mail does have that stealth aspect, which I really like. I value my privacy; I don't necessarily want everybody to know what I'm doing. When you run full- page ads in national magazines, or you have commercials on TV or radio, *everybody* knows what you're doing. When you're using direct mail, you have a lot of privacy. The late, great Gary Halbert used to say that more people will know what you're doing when you run a tiny ad in a national magazine than if you mail 30 million direct mail pieces. Of course, he was being overly-dramatic, but the point is that direct mail is a type of person-to-person communication. **It's a salesperson in an envelope that shows up in your mail box. It's a personal thing between two people, rather than an ad that's broadcast to everyone.**

Now, I don't worry about competition at all; never have, never will. I think worrying about competition is always wrongheaded... but I don't necessarily want all my competitors to know exactly what I'm doing, either. This little local business we're getting ready to start, this pet boutique—well, we have a goal of putting 1,000 of them coast-to-coast. **Our primary marketing vehicle for that store is going to be direct mail,** even though we're going to run space ads in a local newspaper, and we're going to test some radio spot and other media to try to drive people into the store. But once they come to the store, we're going to get their names and addresses and get them on the special discount card program we're putting together; we call it the "Pet Food Club," so they get special discounts every time they buy pet food. At that point, we're going to be very focused on using direct mail to try to get them to come into the store repeatedly. Meanwhile, all that our competitors (and other nosy people) will be able to see are those few small newspaper and radio ads. **Unless they come into our store and get on our mailing list, they're never going to see all the stuff that goes**

on behind the scenes—all the things we're doing to do to stay in touch with those people, to tell them about our special events, our special sales, and all the other efforts we'll make to get those people to give us the names of their friends and family members, so we can send them a nice gift on their behalf.

For a number of years, the national logo for the Direct Mail Association was a circle with two hands clasping: one person to another person. Of course, some young graphic artist sold them on changing it about 20 years ago; but I like the old logo better. I like to think of direct mail as a one-on-one experience. **It's the next best thing to actually going over to someone's house, sitting down with a cup of coffee, and trying to sell them something. It's a personal and private thing.** And it's stealth marketing, because *nobody* else has to know what you're doing.

My colleague Chris Hollinger says he likes to think of each of his direct mail pieces as a jack-in-the-box. As soon as they open the envelope, he pops out, and he's like, "Hi, my name is Chris!" He views the package as his little stealth missile going into their house... and I like that. **Direct mail is very much a one-on-one medium that goes straight into a customer's head, right to where they make their decisions.** It can be used effectively for just about any business, and it really doesn't take that much to differentiate yourself from other people, to out-advertise and out-market them—especially when you use ruthless marketing messages.

Now, direct mail is a humongous industry, and some companies have been sold a bill of goods. They're using the method poorly, because all they want to do is throw some money at it—or worse, they throw some money at another company to do their direct mail for them, and the truth is, that other company probably won't be doing good work most of the time. Unless they're working with a top-notch outfit that actually has some good marketers designing their copy, that copy is going to fall flat with the audience. **That's because no one knows your business like you do, and good direct mail needs to have that personal touch in order to work well.** If you provide it, then regardless of what your business is, **you can use direct mail as a front end system to help carve out more of a market share—to help get people in the door initially, and to keep them coming back.**

So often, this option is overlooked. I think that's mostly because of the postage costs, and the initial costs in general. People can't get beyond that to see the profits possible when direct mail is done properly—so they'll never understand what direct mail really is. **It's not advertising in any traditional way; it's pure salesmanship, because a direct mail package (or series of direct mail packages) can do a very complete job of selling.** If you do your direct mail right, it's like having a top-of-the-line salesperson in an envelope. Everything is there that you would find in the best salesperson—but they'll never call in sick, they'll never go on vacation, and they'll never be caught smoking dope or drinking at lunchtime. They'll never cause you any problems, in fact: they'll just be out there doing their very best, always delivering everything a great salesperson would.

So when you write the sales copy, you try to include the essence of who you are. **You try to let people feel your enthusiasm for what you're selling.**

And in order to improve your direct mail skills, you need to keep swipe files. **A swipe file is a collection of good existing copy by other people, which you can use as models for your own.** So get on mailing lists and start building a swipe file so that you can. When it comes time to create your own direct mail packages, you can use them as a road map, as models for what you want to accomplish. **Don't plagiarize, but look at them for your own needs.** Also, realize that there are a lot of people teaching direct mail now, with plenty of formulas you can use to design and create a winning direct mail package. I've seen dedicated, committed students of marketing use these formulas to create their direct mail packages… but in my opinion, they're just too homogenized, too perfect, too formulated.

Part of what you have to try to do when you create direct mail packages is to include that human quality… and humans aren't perfect. The best *salespeople* aren't perfect. Remember the movie *Planes, Trains & Automobiles* from the 1980s, with John Candy and Steve Martin? Remember John Candy's character? To me, that's the essence of who salespeople are. They're imperfect, yet likable. **They're warm and human… and the best direct mail packages are that way, too. They're not neat, clean and pretty.**

I've got a direct mail package right now that's the dirtiest we've ever mailed. And when I say dirty, I mean, for example, that one paragraph might be half a page long, without any breaks. But, whatever it lacks in beauty, however it violates the rules of proper English, it makes up in enthusiasm and excitement—and it's real. **You know it was written by a real person.** It's not polished; it's not perfect; the language isn't altogether great. **It has that human quality that you would**

find if I came knocking on your door and sat down at your kitchen table to try to sell you something.

Direct mail is simply the most exciting advertising medium ever... **but it's also the most expensive. You can lose money if you're not careful.** But if you do lots of little tests, you could be very aggressive and, at worst, only lose a little money. So test, test, test. Testing is important!

CHAPTER TWO

Always begin with the end in mind.

You work backwards...

☆ First, know what you want to accomplish.

☆ Then decide your starting point — and move forward.

You figure it out, shape it, and fine-tune it as you go!

Always Begin With
The End In Mind

Basically, you start with the end, the desired outcome—that is, your goal—in mind, and then you work backwards. **So first you know what you want to accomplish, then you backtrack to the logical starting point and start moving forward. You figure it out, shape it, and fine tune it as you go.**

Howard Schultz, the CEO of Starbucks, is the perfect example for this chapter. The original Starbucks began in the late 1960s, primarily as a coffee roaster; that is, they roasted fine coffee beans and sold them wholesale to stores that then sold them to consumers, either as beans, grind, or brew. They actually had six company-owned stores where they sold their roasts directly to the public, along with some of the paraphernalia necessary to brew fine coffee. Howard went to work for this company pretty much right after college, learned the business of coffee and coffee roasting, and developed a love and passion for good coffee. If you're a coffee drinker, you understand what that's all about: there's a difference between good and bad coffee, and once you get a taste for the good stuff, you never go back.

Howard had been with the company about 10 years when, at age 34, he got married. He and his wife went to Italy for their honeymoon... and while they were there, Howard saw what's now, essentially, Starbucks. **He saw all these tiny espresso**

shops everywhere in the bigger cities where he and his wife spent the majority of their time. There were dozens and dozens of these little shops, and each had maybe a few hundred regulars at most. The shops were a part of people's everyday life. They all had their favorite little place, and they would go there and meet their friends before going to work, or after work, or during lunch maybe, or during an afternoon break. They served really *good* espresso, but it was also a part of their culture. **Well, Howard came back from his honeymoon fired up, because in his mind he saw the future of Starbucks.**

He was already a top executive for this company, having worked his way up. Now, Starbucks wasn't a big company then: they had under 50 employees, so Howard was able to immediately go to his superiors—people that he liked and trusted, and who liked and trusted him—and say, "This is where we need to take Starbucks. We need to get into the espresso business and start putting these little stores from coast-to-coast. Then, as soon as we conquer America, we need to take this thing abroad. Once we do that, we can build our brand of fine coffee and get it into the stores. Once we do *that*, the potential is unlimited. Who knows what's possible with this thing?"

He was fired up and he was enthusiastic... and to make a long story short, they hated the idea. **They did *not* want to be in that business. No matter how** much he begged and pleaded and tried to get them excited, it was, "No. No. No." They just refused to be in that business. **So Howard had a fateful decision that he had to make: he could either give up his dream, or he could do what he did—which was quit.** Man! Talk about courage! He'd just gotten married. He'd been with this company 10 years... **and he just up and quit rather than give up his dream.**

Then he raised hundreds of thousands of dollars from individual private investors right there in the Seattle area, **and started six little coffee shops of his own, and started making money fulfilling his dream.** The dream was still the same: he wanted to take this thing coast-to-coast and then build it into a worldwide brand. Starbucks was still supplying the coffee, by the way. Well, after just a couple of years of being in that business, **he found out that Starbucks was for sale.** The owners wanted out. Here he was, just a little company with six of these little stores modeled after the ones he'd seen in Italy. Starbucks was a huge company compared to Howard's, and they wanted $3.5 million. Well, Howard didn't have $3.5 million. He'd already borrowed everything he could from everybody he knew just to get started with his six little shops. He'd already tapped out all of his financial sources.

So what did he do? **He spent the entire year of 1986 delivering 242 individual sales presentations.** He got those presentation down to one hour, and during each hour he told the story of Starbucks and how his little company was going to buy Starbucks and then, through the infrastructure that Starbucks had developed since the late 1960s, how he was quickly going to take this thing coast-to-coast. **Then they were going to build a world-wide brand.** They were going to dominate. They were going to get into the grocery stores. They were going to do all kinds of big things.

Those people he spoke to during those 242 presentations in 1986 were doctors, lawyers, accountants and business people—

the folks who had the kind of money he looking for. Almost nine out of 10 people—217—said no. Twenty five people said yes... and we all know how that story ends. **Howard raised the money he needed, he bought Starbucks, and his little company then morphed into the Starbucks of today.** It soon became a billion-dollar-a-year company. Many of those early investors put up just $100,000 each... and those investments quickly turned into over $10 million each.

I find that hugely exciting! Think about how *foolish* those 217 people who said no to him feel today. Some of them probably can't even drive by a Starbucks without getting sick to their stomachs because they said no to Howard. So how does this story relate to my point here? **Well, every entrepreneur has a dream—but few are willing to go out on a limb as Howard did, starting with the end in mind and believing in the dream so much that he quit his job despite his brand new wife and all kinds of uncertainties.** And now, of course, Howard is a billionaire—one of the richest men in the country. He began with the end in mind. **He had a vision, and that vision became the roadmap he followed to success.** At that point, it was just a matter of trying to figure out how to accomplish it.

He started with the end in mind and kept it firmly in mind. When he made his one hour sales presentation to the potential investors, he was sharing that end goal with them, telling them what he envisioned for this company. Twenty five of those people caught the vision and had the courage to go with him. The other 217 people didn't. They didn't believe in him, and they surely didn't believe in his dream. They were locked into this whole idea of, "Who in their right mind is going to pay $4 for a fancy cup of coffee?"

But Howard saw it; and a few other people saw it with him. **Having that end goal, that end vision, motivated him.** Until then, Howard never even considered himself to be a salesman. He *learned* how to be a salesperson by delivering this presentation again and again, and he got really good at it. What he never got good at was how every time somebody said no, it was like getting hit in the stomach. Then he'd have to muster up all his courage and give the next presentation... and he had to do it with just as much enthusiasm as he had the last five times, when somebody said no to him. **By keeping that end goal in mind, he really did help to keep his enthusiasm high; and this ultimately led him to achieve that end goal, with the help of a lot of other good, talented people.**

Howard is an excellent example of a visionary who saw something that *could* be, and went about challenging people's thinking on it. Sure, a lot of those people laughed. Many others blew him off and said, "It can't be done." A lot of people refused to join him, and yet he had some who caught the vision and did join him, and the rest is business history. And yes, Howard and his crew did take the business worldwide. When Chris Lakey was in China recently, he had some Starbucks coffee—and he says it tasted the same as it does here. It's Starbucks wherever it is. People appreciate that consistency, just like they appreciate the way that McDonald's tastes the same wherever you are.

The model works. Chris says he was near three Starbucks' stores most of the time he was in China. There was one right across the street from his hotel, and another one, ten miles away, at a place where he had to be a few times during his trip. So, Starbucks was always close while he was there... and yes, it's an expensive cup of coffee even in China. The model's the same whether it's around the corner from your house here in the States or whether it's in China or anywhere else. **They've done a good job, and his vision for that was a big part of their entire story.**

Beginning with the end in mind and working backwards from that point all starts with figuring out what you want to accomplish as your ultimate end game. From that point, you figure out how to make it be what you want it to be. Consider a professional football team, which has in its sights the season ahead. Let's just talk about the coach. I'm not even going to go into general management and the owner of the team, who really look beyond the season, planning on several years down the road. Their goals are bigger than just the upcoming season. I know that coaches do that, too, but let's look at the immediate example of a single season. When it's springtime in the NFL and a football team is looking at what it wants to accomplish this season, they start by looking at the Super Bowl. That's their ultimate goal; every team wants to play in and win the Super Bowl. Some teams have realistic expectations or goals to make the Super Bowl, some don't, but every team wants it. And they prepare for that goal.

How do you get to the Super Bowl, and hopefully bring your team a victory trophy? How does that happen? **You start with the end in mind.** In the spring, just a couple of months after the last Super Bowl's over and you're all sitting in your spring meetings, you begin your preparations. When you begin physical training, you're preparing physically for the challenges of the upcoming season. You're building muscle tone, losing weight, and otherwise getting your physique ready for a 16-game regular season. That carries through to summer camp, where you learn your playbook and hone your ability to work as a team. Preseason games start in August; they don't count for the Super Bowl, so basically, you're training on the field against other teams. You're evaluating the situation, and the coaches are making decisions on who's going to be the best set of 53 guys to take them to their goal of winning the Super Bowl. Eventually, the season begins, and now they're playing real games. **The goal is still there, but they've now moved on to the implementation phase.**

So they play all 16 games of the regular season, and by the end they've hopefully won enough games to either win their division or get a wild card position in the playoffs. From there, they try to win each playoff game, so they can make it to the Super Bowl, and then hopefully win that. **All these things happen because they set that goal at the beginning of the year that they wanted *this* year to be the year they won it all.** They try that every year, and only one team wins; but every team has to aspire for it, and they set their seasons up as if they're going to make it happen. Everything they do is an attempt to see that actually happen.

It always starts with the end goal, and then you work from there to figure out what it's going to take. In order to make the Super Bowl, you have to make the playoffs. In order to make the playoffs, you have to win 10 or more football games during the course of the year. What are you going to do to win

10 games? That starts with the off-season program that helps you acquire the players you need; then you build the right schemes to try on the field; then you start physical training; and it moves forward from there.

In business, it's pretty much the same way. You start with the end in mind, and everything you do involves working towards that goal in some way. That's why the worst thing you can do is live your business life in a haphazard, helter-skelter mode, where you just float around from day to day, and some days you do things, and other days you don't. You just float by, and pretty soon you're at the end—and you don't really know what you've accomplished. Ultimately, you regret that you didn't develop a better game plan, or you didn't set your goals in a more proper way. You don't want things to be like that in the end. And by the way, that "end" doesn't have to be the end of your physical life; rather, it might be the end of the 10-year business plan, or even of a particular promotion.

Events are a good fit for this model, because if you have a goal to put on the biggest and best event you've ever done, you have to be specific. What does that look like? Let's say you want to have 1,000 people sitting in a conference room in this hotel, in this city, on this date. That's your end goal. Well, what are you going to do to achieve that goal? Where do you need to be three months before the event? Where do you need to be six months before the event? Everything you do is oriented toward, focused on, the single task of getting people to buy tickets to attend your event, because you have a goal of putting 1,000 butts in the seats. If you stray from that, then you lose sight of that goal and end up not achieving those results. **It all starts**

with that end deadline, followed by what you do during the interim period to help you reach that goal.

Now, many people are absolutely terrified to set huge goals, mostly because they don't have all the details figured out from the word go; they want to wait and try to figure everything out before they start. They're afraid to go out there unprepared, uncertain of knowing exactly what's going to happen. That's self-defeating. **You can't be afraid of any of this; you've got to be willing to figure everything out as you go along. That's why you set the goals first.** If you want to travel to another city 3,000 miles away, you first get that destination in mind, and then you try to figure out how to get there: which highways you're going to take, where you're going to stop along the way, and all of that kind of stuff. You just have to have faith that you'll make it. You know that if the car breaks down, you've got AAA.

Your best ideas come to you while you're in the heat of it all. You figure things out as you go, and you cross the bridges when you get to them. You can't be afraid to do any of this. It's like driving at night: even on the darkest of nights, if you're on a reasonably good road, and you're driving in a reasonably good car, and the weather conditions are decent, all you have to do is be able to see in front of you just a few hundred feet. If you do that, you can get exactly where you want to go.

Your best ideas come to you while you're moving forward. So many people are stalled because they're waiting to come up with the perfect idea... **but the perfect ideas don't start out that way full-blown. They come through the process of moving forward.** You're rarely, if ever, going to get the perfect ideas from the beginning, if only because the really good ideas come in the heat of the moment, when you're actually fulfilling on your ideas for the marketplace—because you're going to encounter certain problems that you didn't expect in the beginning, and didn't think through back then. Trust me on this: everything has to be developed constantly, in response to the people you're selling it to. Great ideas don't just happen in a vacuum; things continue to develop, and idea number 27 grows out of the previous 26 ideas. **You're constantly improving things, getting better, because the ideas take shape as you move forward.**

I usually try to give myself plenty of time for a project. If I have to write a big sales letter, I'll allow myself a couple weeks just to do all the raw writing that has to be done—and when I say raw, I'm talking about no real editing. A lot of the time I write in these huge blocks, without paragraph breaks and proper grammar. I just write. I just try to stay focused on the benefits, writing as persuasively as I know how to—and I don't question what I do. **I just put the pedal to the metal and write. Every day I work on it a little, and I commit to it.**

I know that the best ideas will come to me on day four or day five... or even, as in the earlier example several Ways back, on day six and seven. Ultimately, I might use just very little of what I wrote on those first few days, since **most of what ends up in a sales letter all came on the last few days. That's when my mind was on fire.** That was when the flow of ideas was unimpeded, when I'd gotten rid of the mental debris choking the outflow. **When people get the finished sales letter, they won't realize that this was what the process was like.** The writing is full of enthusiasm. The ideas have been developed, and it's much more persuasive. They see very little of the first 3,000-5,000 words I wrote. They just see the last 3,000-5,000 words, because that's the part that matters.

So many people are just sitting on their butts, waiting for everything to develop completely. They want everything to be perfect, and it's been my experience that they end up hurting themselves. As Voltaire once pointed out, "the perfect is the enemy of the good." **If you procrastinate because you're aiming for perfection, you won't get anything done! The *real* concept here is ready, aim, fire—and keep firing.** The worst thing you can do is sit around and wait for perfect conditions or perfect timing, or otherwise have a goal but no plan for moving forward. **Answers come as you fight through the clutter.**

I think that many times, people are gripped by fear. They're either afraid of making a mistake, of saying the wrong thing, or of doing something that doesn't end with a pot of gold at the end of the rainbow. **I think people hurt themselves by not taking action.** So please, don't be afraid of not having all the answers. **The answers will come in time as you move forward.** As the old Nike slogan says, "Just Do It." Don't put it off until everything's just right. **If you'll just get out there and start working towards your goals, clarity will happen.** It may not happen quickly, and there may be a lot of fuzziness at first—but eventually the clouds will break, and the sunlight will pour through. It'll be like one of those bright, sunny days after a rain.

You wake up, and you see the sun in the sky, and you feel the warmth. It feels good on your skin. Well, working on a project can be like that. You just move forward with your end in mind, overcoming the cloudy conditions until you finally break through to the sunny weather. That's what it feels like to have these breakthrough moments where you feel the productivity take shape as your ideas go from abstract to specific, as you see a project come together and move towards completion. **It feels good. It makes you feel you've accomplished something.** You feel productive, and you're moving that much closer to your goal.

You've got to just keep moving forward to get there. It's not like you can go to bed for a week when it gets cloudy; you keep getting up, and you keep going through your routine, pushing on through. You know that sunshine is eventually going to happen, and you're just waiting for it to come through so you can celebrate. **On every single business-related project, if it's big enough, there's always a period of time when you'll have your regrets, when you'll wish you'd never have started it.** You'll be frustrated and confused; you'll feel like crap, and you'll wish you could back out. **But once you've been involved in enough projects, you'll reach a really cool place where you realize that all these terrible emotions are ephemeral.** You've been there and done that a bunch of times, so you just know that this too shall pass.

That's one thing that comes from a little experience. Those people who don't have experience may not realize that it *will* pass, that if they just keep moving forward, they'll get beyond it. You know, as a copywriter, I used to be *so* intimidated when I looked at some of the beautiful sales letters out there. But back then, I didn't realize the amount of rewriting, editing, time and hard work that it took to develop those letters. Now that I write my own sales letters and put them out there, I suspect that there are other people trying to learn our craft who are looking at our stuff and saying, "Oh man, those guys are great!" They don't realize that it may have taken us two or three weeks, or in some cases two or three months, to put that letter together, and during most of that time it didn't look *anything* like the finished project.

So don't be intimidated! I wish I'd known all this when I first got started, because I would have saved myself a lot of heartache. **That's one thing I want to pass along: don't give up!** If you start with the end in mind and work steadily toward it, you *will* eventually break through into the sunlight!

CHAPTER THREE

A good direct mail offer is nothing more than <u>a</u> <u>salesman</u> <u>in</u> <u>an</u> <u>envelope</u>.

The really cool thing is:

You can have thousands of these little salesmen working for you every single day!

A Salesman in an Envelope

A great direct mail offer is nothing more than a salesman in an envelope. **The really cool thing here is you can have *thousands* of these little salesmen working for you every single day, knocking on doors and building the case for your product or service.** They do this without them asking for time off, or calling in sick, or causing problems, or any number of other issues that you might have with a real salesman. Salesmen need a lot of hand-holding, sometimes. It takes quite a bit of skill to manage a sales department... but you don't have to do that if you can just put together a good direct mail letter. That letter can become the equivalent of the best possible salesman.

This concept can make you millions of dollars—which I know for a fact is true, because we've done it here at M.O.R.E., Inc. We started out with space advertising in September 1988, with a couple of small ads. We pyramided the profits, and then we started running some full-page ads, and we did fairly well. **But it wasn't until we started mailing direct mail pieces that our income really shot through the roof!**

When we met our mentor, Russ Von Hoelscher, we'd been in business about six months, running space ads exclusively. We were generating about $500 a day in gross revenue. Within nine months of hiring Russ as our marketing consultant, our income jumped from about $16,000 a month to almost $100,000 a *week* in total sales. I'm not trying to brag on us here; if anything, I'm bragging on Russ, because he was instrumental in helping us pull this off. Now, what did he do? **He helped us take something that was already working and make it work much better.** He just poured jet fuel on an existing fire.

Russ had over 20 years of experience in the business at that time. He knew exactly what to do and how to do it. He told us all the things we needed to do to improve what we were doing, but the one thing that helped us more than anything else was that he got us involved in direct mail marketing. **Once we started using direct mail, our income skyrocketed.** Soon, we were bringing in millions of dollars a year. Within five years, we had generated over $10 million in total revenue, and we've never looked back.

Now, admittedly, direct mail is one of the more expensive ways to market your products and services—and this is where a lot of people fail. If you don't do it just right, you're going to lose your money very quickly. I'll talk about how to do it properly later in this chapter, and provide some pointers because I assure you, **this method works well, in large part because it replaces the trouble and expense of live salesmen.**

There are many definitions of selling, but I like to think of it as a performance. Recently, I was walking on my treadmill, watching one of my favorite rock 'n' roll acts— Aerosmith, the Americanized version of the Rolling Stones. I was watching Steven Tyler in the *River of Life* presentation, and the guy is one hell of a performer. Even if you don't like the music, all you have to do is just watch the guy. He's constantly in motion, getting people excited. He's dancing around on the stage, getting people pumped up. He's performing. Performing is about getting people excited, making them feel it, drawing them in, holding them to the edge of their seats, captivating them, entertaining them, making them want to know more.

A good salesperson is a performer. They may not be jumping up and down—in fact, some of the best performances are understated a bit—but they're making you want to know more. they're getting you excited. They know exactly what to say, and how to say it. **Well, you can incorporate all those elements into a good direct mail package and captivate people the same way.** When you make them excited, you can build your case for your offer and get people to see that what you have for them is worth far more than the money you're asking in exchange. That's the secret here: you have to build a solid case for what you're offering. **Your offer has to make people feel like when they get to the end of your sales letter, they almost can't contain themselves.** It's irresistible: they just have to have whatever it is that you're offering. **A good salesperson does that, but so does a good direct mail presentation.**

To be truly effective, any sales presentation must involve a transference of emotion, and a transference of belief. The more you believe in what you're doing, and the more you present it in just the right way to just the right people, the more it's like opening up a giant safe. If you get all the numbers right, then the tumblers inside the lock will move a certain way, and it clicks. You pull the level and open the door, and all that money inside that safe is yours! **That's a great metaphor for what happens when you can put together a direct mail package that models a great salesperson.**

STEALTH MARKETING!

Now, the good news is that you can spend weeks and even months developing your direct mail package. It doesn't need to happen all at once. I just got done late yesterday afternoon with a 44-page sales letter that I've been working on for about three weeks now—some days for a couple of hours, some days for four or five hours. Toward the end, over the last three days, I spent much more time on it. Yesterday I spend six or seven hours; the two days before that, I spent 10 hours each.

So, I've put a lot of hours into this thing, but now it's finished. It's part of a special opportunity that we're using two-step marketing with. First, we mail a four-page sales letter with a one-page order form to the prospect. **This gives them the gist of the offer, and lets them send in for this 44-page report.** Along with this report, there will be an audio CD that Chris and I produced, where we go over the special report page by page.

So we're doing a complete sales presentation on a two-step marketing model, where we're trying to separate the smaller core of people who are more serious and better qualified from the larger herd of people who aren't. We're trying to pre-qualify them a bit, and once we do that, it's Katie-bar-the-door—because think about it, a 44-page sales letter! I asked Chris Lakey to look it all over this morning. It might take him two or three hours to get through it, because it's a long sales presentation. But again, we're trying to ask people to give us a lot of money—anywhere from $1,000 to $10,000. In our market, that's a fortune.

If you're asking for that kind of money, you'd better deliver a pretty solid performance. **You'd better present all the benefits clearly and run through all the objections.** You'd better make a strong case for why people should purchase what you're offering. Again, you're trying to get people to see what you want them to see. **You're trying to convey your beliefs to them, so they can see that the benefits you're offering are worth much more than the money you're asking in return.** That was the goal of that 44-page letter. It's the goal of *every* direct mail package that we do.

The letter I just finished is, I believe, an effective sales presentation, and it's one that took me several weeks of work. **I just kept writing and writing, and then I boiled it down.** Believe me, that 44 pages started out as about 150 pages! Some of those 100+ pages that didn't make it to the final letter may make it into the follow-up marketing that we'll do. That text can still be used for lots of different things... but the point is you can take as much time as you want to develop something like this.

Heck, even *now* this letter might not be done. Chris or I will probably eventually do version number two. Instead of being 44 pages, it may end up being 36 pages. And maybe version number three will only be 32 pages; but eventually, we'll get this thing fine-tuned to our satisfaction. **Ultimately, using a combination of the right two-step marketing strategy along with this long-form sales letter, our work could deliver millions of dollars for the company.** It's happened to us many times over the years. The first time it happened it just shocked us. It was like Christmas when you were a kid. The second time it happened, it was very exciting. Now, it's kind of commonplace. I don't mean to brag; I'm just saying that the more you do this, the more typical it becomes. It's still exciting, don't get me wrong; but after a while, you get used to it, and that's a great thing.

Look, don't envy us our success. **Join us! You can create good direct mail promotions that emulate everything that a good salesperson can do.** They get people interested initially. They do all the pre-qualifying that a salesperson normally does on a cold call. Your direct mail piece can deliver an effective sales presentation; you can use audio with it, or you can use a live salesperson with it, too. That's what we do with all our direct mail packages. If people still have questions after they read it all, they can call and talk to a real salesperson. We have those elements, and then we follow up. We put a lot of time and money and effort into all our follow-up marketing because every great salesperson knows that just because somebody says, "No," once, twice, three times, or four times doesn't mean that they won't say, "Yes," on the sixth or seventh or eighth time. **Our direct mail follow-ups are trying to keep knocking on the door. They keep trying to get people interested, and keep trying to get them to come around.**

It's very powerful when done right. There are people out there who are making the kind of money that makes our success pale by comparison, so again, don't think I'm bragging. We've made millions at this, **but some people have made hundreds of millions or *billions* using good, old-fashioned direct mail combined with other media.** I talked about the audio; well, you can use the Internet, too. Your direct mail piece can do all kinds of things, and have all kinds of power.

The subject of direct mail is something that Chris Lakey and I have both spent a lot of time studying. **It's the bread and butter of our business, and the foundation of everything we**

teach. As you may have noticed, a big portion of this book is dedicated to the concept of direct mail and everything that goes into it. This particular strategy is just one of many that outline what makes direct mail a success.

So let me emphasize again: direct mail lets you have many thousands or even *millions* of these little salespeople working for you every single day that the mail is delivered. Even on Sundays, you still have the opportunity to have your envelopes opened, your sales presentation made, and hopefully—if all goes well—the opportunity for people to follow your instructions and place their orders. And by the way, these days, "mail order" doesn't necessarily have to mean *ordering* by mail. **Direct mail just means that *delivery* is by mail. The response mechanism could be by phone, fax, mail, or Internet.** That's just how you start the process. **The actual mail offer grabs their interest, and then you deliver by mail.**

It all begins with that salesperson in an envelope.

Let's say you had the ability to send live salespeople door-to-door all over town, or all over your state, or all over the country, and they're all knocking on doors for you. Hopefully, a person will open the door; hopefully, they won't see the salesperson and slam the door in their face immediately. Ideally, that salesperson will say something to them that makes the prospect feel like they at least need to give the salesperson a few minutes, and the prospect lets them in. The salesperson does their presentation, and at the end of the presentation, they've convinced the prospect that your product is worth the money you're asking them to spend on it. They give the salesperson the money in exchange for the product, and the salesman goes to the next house, and on and on. The right company could have thousands of these salespeople all over the country making sales. This has been an effective model for marketing for decades, and it's the way that some stuff is still sold today, although you don't see it as much as you used to.

Chris Lakey moved back to the city just over six months ago; prior to that, he and his family lived out in the country. He tells me that he didn't get any door-to-door salespeople when he was in the country—whether it was because they thought Chris had a shotgun trained on them, or just didn't want to bother people, or that the area was just rural enough that it wasn't worth their time to go door-to-door. In fact, the only time someone came to his door in the country, they wanted him to go to a political rally, and he was pretty shocked at that. Well, now that he's back in the city, he's had a number of people come selling door-to-door. **The interesting thing about a door-to-door salesperson is that, often, they'll make a pretty convincing case if you actually listen to them**—which is why a lot of people don't answer the door, because they know they're susceptible to sales pressure from a person who's actually standing in front of them.

It's much easier to hang up the phone on a telemarketer, or to decide whether you want to read a sales letter. You don't offend the marketer if you don't read the letter. **A door-to-door salesperson is a little more difficult to turn down,** especially if they've shown you pictures of their kids and they tell you what they're doing with the money. Usually, they make a convincing case, and they often demonstrate the product for you, walking you through why you should have it.

A few months back, a gentleman approached Chris selling some kind of $40 cleaning solution in a bottle. He cleaned the plastic cover over the headlight of Chris's car, cleaned the driveway, and even cleaned the glass on the front door of the house. He was showing Chris all these things you could do with the solution, just outside of the house; he didn't even come in. He said, "You don't know me from Adam. I don't want to come into your house, but let me show you a few things it can do right out here in your driveway," and made a convincing case. In the end, it's hard to say no to someone like that. They've done a good job of presenting the reasons why you need the product, even when you didn't know you did before. **They tell you what problems or challenges it solves, and in the end they make a case for why you should write a check to them.** That's what a good door-to-door salesperson will do for a company.

Well, think of direct mail as a variation of that classic door-to-door salesmanship. What you're looking at doing here is replacing that need to pay a commission to a door-to-door salesperson, the need for insurance and sick days and dealing with personality issues. **A direct mail offer really is the next best thing to having a sales force going door-to-door.** You're sending out an entire sales presentation inside an envelope, or in a box, or in a package, depending on how you deliver it.

A direct mail package could contain a DVD, video presentation, an audio CD that presents a message that they listen to, or a mix of the above, all in addition to a sales letter. There are all kinds of ways that you can use that direct mail package to convey your sales message. **The entire presentation that could be made in person via a salesperson**

can be made with a sales package. I talked earlier about my 44-page sales letter. Well, as you can imagine, a 44-page sales letter isn't something that you can quickly read through, and decide whether you're interested in the product or not. You may scan the first page to decide if you want to read the letter or not, but you don't get the whole story by spending three minutes with a 44-page letter. It takes you a while to get through that, just like it takes a while for a door-to-door salesperson to make an effective presentation. They come into your home, and they demo the product on your floor or whatever they're trying to sell. It might take an hour for you get through that, just like it might take about an hour to get through a 44-page sales letter, maybe even longer.

If you include a DVD or CD, maybe you've got an hour-long presentation that you make that way. It takes time to sell your product or your service. **Sure, there's material that goes in your direct mail package that replaces the need for a door-to-door salesperson, but you tell the same story, doing all the things that you might do if you were standing in front of somebody.**

When you write a sales letter, it's most effective to write as if you're speaking to one person. The tone of your letter, the words you use — it's as if you're sitting right across the table from somebody and sharing with them all the reasons why they need to own your product or service, and why they should be looking to receive the benefits that your offer can provide to them. Your writing style needs to reflect that one-on-one tone, which is why in the best scenarios, your direct mail letter can have a feel of an actual salesperson standing in front of the prospect. **The tone is the same as the tone you would take if you were there in person.** The words you use, the stories you tell, the offer you make, it's all the same. You're just writing it instead of delivering it face-to-face.

Depending on your company, how well your offer works, and how many prospects you have to deliver it to, you may have thousands or millions of these salesmen in an envelope out there, doing their jobs. You send them out into the mail stream, generally first class or bulk if you're mailing a lot of packages. **Delivery is fairly consistent; you know, in general, how long it's going to take before it arrives at the person's home or office; and you know that within a certain period of time, you can expect results from that mailing.** Instead of waiting for your sales team to deliver the results of, "I knocked on this many doors. I had this many slammed in my face. This many people let me in. This many people said yes. This many people brought it," you get the results immediately, because your fax machine is ringing, the calls are coming in, the forms are coming in the mail: the orders are piling up. You sit back and analyze the results, and your business is profitable or not based on the success or failure of that direct mail offer.

Using a direct mail package can replace an entire department of door-to-door salespeople. Sure, there's an administrative process here, and you have to pay a mailing house or someone to manage the mailings for you. Then you have to deal with the orders. But you don't worry about dealing with an entire staff of paid salespeople who are going door-to-door for you, and mileage, and wear and tear on the vehicles— all those kinds of things if you're using direct mail. **If you're**

doing your mailing right, you're delivering your offer straight into the hands of your targeted audience in a cost-effective way. Direct mail is anything but cheap; but it *can* be very cost effective, and your return on your investment can be very high if you have a mailing with the right offer reaching the right people at the right time.

The basics of salesmanship in print are pretty simple. If you do it right, it's an investment towards future profits, rather than a cost. And you can keep it small, too, if you like. You don't have to go out there and risk a whole bunch of money all at once. **Test small, and then take the ideas that work the best and roll them out.** That way, you only spend real money once you've completed a series of smaller and more inexpensive tests, proving what works best and what doesn't. The one big mistake that so many people make with direct mail is that they do what P.T. Barnum called "trying to catch a whale using a minnow for bait." I love that quote, because it represents to me the biggest mistake made in direct mail marketing. **Everybody wants the huge results, but they don't want to put in the time, and the work, and the effort, and the *money* to get those big results.** Case in point: this 44-page sales letter that's sitting on Chris's desk right now.

A lot of people don't want to spend the money to print up something that's 44 pages long, so they'll only do a 15- or 20-page letter instead. Well, something like that doesn't do a complete job of selling. They're trying to get big results with a small letter—i.e., trying to catching the whale by using a minnow as bait. If they do make money, they never make as much money as they *could*, if only they were thinking like a salesperson.

As the owner of a company, you don't tell a salesperson to stop talking after five minutes. **You tell them to do whatever it takes to get the sale.** It may take them an hour, it may take them two hours, or it may take them three weeks of calling back the prospect and continuing to answer the questions before you finally get that sale. **The same principles apply for all good direct response types of marketing.**

CHAPTER FOUR

Enthusiasm Sells!

If you're excited about what you do — it will attract others... People will gather around to watch you burn!

Enthusiasm makes up for all kinds of defects! After all, everyone loves a truly enthusiastic person.

$ $ $ $ $

To be a super-salesperson you have to believe strongly in whatever you are selling.

Selling is a transference of emotion! You must be sold <u>before</u> you can sell!

Enthusiasm Sells!

If you're excited about what you do, it's going to attract other people. As the famous minister (I believe it was John Wesley) once said, "Catch yourself on fire and they'll gather around to watch you burn." Enthusiasm is sort of like a fire. Sure, it's a spirit, it's an attitude; but it's warm like a fire, too. **When you're using it in a sales presentation, it makes up for all kinds of other deficits and liabilities.** You could take a salesperson who's not very trained or polished, or who hasn't spent a lot of time preparing or doesn't have any other real skills, and give them enthusiasm—and they can do a much better job than somebody who made the exact presentation perfectly but without passion.

That's what enthusiasm is: it's a passion, it's a fire, it's an energy, it's an excitement. The best sales people know how to project it. They know how to put it out there. Don't think that they were born that way, because they weren't; and don't assume that they're not working their asses off when they deliver this hard core sales presentation, because they're working *very* hard. People just don't realize it.

I had a guy who worked for us about 10 years ago, and he saw a presentation at one of our seminars. Later, he told me how much he would like to be able to do something like that some day. I was trying to encourage him, trying to tell him that he could do it. He said, "No, TJ, I could never do what you do. I'm just not that enthusiastic." We were just having a conversation and all of a sudden, just to prove my point, I went into my sales pitch mode. I said, "What do you mean? You don't have my enthusiasm? You mean, you're not like this," and I started talking really fast, putting passion into my words. Then I started jumping up and down a little bit and waving my arms like I do in front of a group.

He probably thought I was just being a jerk, but what I was trying to convey was that you can learn to turn it on and off. It's not that I'm being fake and phony when I do this, because I really do have enthusiasm for what I sell; otherwise, I couldn't sell it. But as I discussed earlier, **selling is a performance—and the best performers put some energy into their presentations.** They don't put you to sleep. Just think of the very best presentations you've ever seen, whether political or religious or business-related. It can even come from your own personal life. Maybe somebody had something they really wanted to get across to you, and they said it in a forceful way. **They put some power and energy into it, and** *that* **is enthusiasm.**

There is such a thing as quiet enthusiasm. In fact, some of the best sales presentations I've seen haven't been all that exciting, but boy, they made me stand in line with my money. Here's what it represented: the solid belief of the salesperson who was delivering that presentation. **They were 100% confident about what they were selling, and that's part of what enthusiasm is.**

When you're around somebody enthusiastic, you're

basically caught up in their total certainty. **They completely believe in what they're doing.** So just because some people don't jump up and down and do stuff like that doesn't mean they're not enthusiastic. They still have this very quiet sense of total belief in what they're presenting, this attractive 100% certainty. That's really what people are looking for, especially because they have so many choices and so many confusing statements. We're living in an age where there are many choices available for almost everything, and there are so many more people saying so many different things. **So when somebody stands up and communicates in a forceful, confident way, using enthusiasm and belief in their presentation, they're more likely to grab your attention.** You can just tell how sold they are on what they're doing.

Look at what the opposite of what enthusiasm is; that's where you can really get a sense of what this word means. Think about people who are bored and lifeless. You want to put a mirror up to their faces just to see if they're even breathing, right? They're apathetic, moving very slowly. **Think of all of the qualities of the most unenthusiastic, boring person you could possibly imagine, and realize that this thing called enthusiasm is precisely the opposite of that.**

Again, it doesn't have to be jumping up and down or anything like that—but it *is* a sense that the person is totally alive, and they totally believe in what they're saying. and so they're very, very convincing—and that transfers over to you. **Selling is the transfer of emotion, and so you have to be sold yourself before you can sell to others.** This is one of the keys to enthusiasm. I was a salesman for quite a while before I started doing halfway decent with it. The first few years I barely even survived; and not that I was phenomenally successful when I *did* start succeeding, **but the first real success I had as a salesperson came when I started selling something that I really, truly believed in.**

I'm not saying that I didn't have my bad days, and I'm not saying that I made a million dollars overnight. That came later. But I started experiencing real success when I believed in what I was presenting to people. I was deeply committed to what I was doing, and I knew I was good. That was when I had my first business, my carpet cleaning service. I was confident that I could do the job, and that I could do a better job than my competition for less money. **I conveyed that to people.** If they gave me a chance to get inside their house, look out, because I was going to walk out with some of their cash!

That was pretty much my attitude, and my closing ratio was high if I could just get inside somebody's house and get a bid. Once I did, I could close more than one out of two deals. Some days I could close two out of three. I'm not saying that to brag; the point is, the challenge was to get inside their house to get the bid. **I was enthusiastic, I had that passion for what I was doing, that fire that people take to.** It's not something you're born with—though sure, some people have a better aptitude for it than others, just as some people are more gifted mathematically or musically. **Yet it's something that anybody can develop, if they just get out there and try.**

This is true even of people who are more mild-mannered than me, and I would include Chris Lakey on that list. For the most part, Chris Lakey is a very quiet individual. But if you get him talking about politics, look out! Recently we did a presentation in Dallas, Texas where we started to talk about politics, and we were going around in a group. On Chris's second presentation, he was standing up waving his arms, and people were practically afraid of him. The two people sitting on either side of him just kind of eased their chairs away, like they thought he was going to pick up a chair and start throwing it around. He was totally passionate about his subject!

Enthusiasm, I think, is all about finding that thing that you really, really believe in and tapping into that horsepower. In the last chapter, we talked about door-to-door salespeople. I think one of the reasons some door-to-door salespeople are good at what they do is that they have plenty of enthusiasm. They get you all excited about whatever they're selling. **That excitement transfers from the seller, them, to the buyer, you, and makes you want to own whatever they're selling.** When you go to fairs or flea markets or conventions where you see people with booths who are selling products, sometimes you see the same thing. The booths doing the best are the ones where there's an enthusiastic salesperson at the counter, and they're excited to be telling you all about their product. Whether they're faking it or it's sincere, that enthusiasm comes through, and it's transferred to the person on the receiving end of that presentation.

If you're excited about what you do, or excited about what you're selling, it naturally attracts other people. People want to see what's going on. They want to see what all the excitement is about. You see this sometimes at events where there's actually a salesperson—a booth where they're selling some type of kitchen gadget or something. People are watching, and there's a lot of noise and commotion, and pretty soon there are more people gathered and there's some energy and excitement there, and you want to check out what's going on. More people gather. Pretty soon, there's a big crowd, because they hear the excitement in the existing crowd and they see the excitement up on stage.

That enthusiasm attracts other people. **In its more basic nature, it's the difference between a positive, out-going person and a grump.** Who would you rather be around: someone who's grumpy all the time, or someone who has a jovial personality? You'd almost always rather be around someone who's fun, someone who makes you laugh, right? **There's an attractor factor there. It's the same with enthusiasm.** It's a natural attractant, and people are enticed by it. They're excited to be around it.

Even a bad salesperson can find some level of success if they're enthusiastic. You could even be wrong, and be exciting and enthusiastic, and have a group of people believe you and follow you—even though what you're saying isn't correct. I suppose I could even make up some kind of lie and tell it to the people around me with a certain level of enthusiasm, and they would believe me. Now, they would only believe me the *first* time; especially, for example, if I told them the building was on fire and they needed to run. But once they realized that the building was not in fact on fire, they might yell at me. Then they would go about their day, and wouldn't believe anything I said ever again. But the first time, I could sell it, because I was enthusiastic—even though I wasn't telling the truth.

The point is, your enthusiasm will go a long way toward getting people to believe what you're saying. You're excited about it—and your story has credibility, in part, because of that. You see this with everyday life quite often. For example: even a bad salesperson might be really good at selling a cell phone. They might talk to their friends about their new iPhone or Droid and how it's the greatest phone of all time. They'll be excited and enthusiastic while they talk to their friends about someone else's product. Or maybe they'll tell you about this TV show they watch, and how exciting it is. Or they'll tell you about this new widget they have that does this or that, or about their favorite restaurant. **They'll promote other people's products with enthusiasm, and people will purchase those products or services because of it.**

Let's say I'm excited about this great Mexican restaurant I just ate at last night, and I'm really enthusiastic about it. I can tell you why their chips and salsa are the best I've ever had, and how their guacamole makes your mouth water. It's just so good! And you have to try their dessert, because the dessert just makes it even better. If I go into all this detail, and I'm enthusiastic as I describe this restaurant, as long as you like Mexican you're probably going to try it out.

But even people who are enthusiastic in everyday situations, and are used to sharing things that they're involved with on a daily basis with their friends or family, often can't convey that enthusiasm when they get into sales situations. They struggle with selling, when all they really need (assuming they've got a good product) is a little enthusiasm. They need to be able to convince people that they're excited for their product or service, and that the prospect should *also* get excited. **In order to do that, you have to start with a belief in what you're selling.** If you don't believe in what you're selling, it's hard to manufacture enthusiasm.

Oh, it can be done, and you've probably seen people do it. Sometimes that can work, but I think for maximum effectiveness, the salesperson has to believe in what they're selling. They have to believe that the recipient is going to receive the benefits they're promoting; if they do, then they're going to transfer that enthusiasm more effectively. **You've got to start with the belief that what you're selling is legitimate, that what you're selling is good and real and will provide value to the prospect.** Transferring that emotion becomes your chief goal; and to transfer that emotion, you've got to first be able to be enthusiastic.

It's like an electric charge. If there's no electric charge on your end, you can't shock somebody. If you're not excited, if you're not enthusiastic, there's no way to get them excited and enthusiastic about it. You've got to get all charged up yourself, and then you can touch somebody, spread that enthusiasm to them, get them excited. **Once they're excited, they're ready to make a purchase. That's what enthusiasm is all about.**

Now, you can practice getting excited; you can get better at it. This doesn't mean you're faking it; you're just taking natural behavior that you already have and cranking up the volume full blast. There are *so* many people who are afraid to let their enthusiasm show, because they don't want to seem fake. But face the fact that it's all about performing; and in order to perform effectively, you've got to step it up a little bit, move a little bit. You have to make people feel it. So get past all your ideas about this being phony. **You *can* practice getting excited, you *can* practice projecting your personality, and as long as it really is a part of you and you're just cranking up the volume, then you're not being a phony.** You're still being yourself, only full blast.

This is easiest when you sell things that you honestly, truly believe in; and that's what you should try to do. Your ability to believe in things is limited, of course; there are some things you'll never believe in, some lines that you'll just never cross. **That's good: it makes you a person of character.** You have rules for yourself, things that you will and won't do. And yet so many things can fall in between the two extremes. You can make yourself believe in things; the same way you sell to somebody else, you can sell yourself. That's critical, because again, you must be sold first before you can sell to somebody else.

One of the secrets of the people who perform best in sales environments, especially when they're up in front of a crowd, is that **they spend a lot of time thinking about what they're selling.** They've taken the time necessary to convince themselves that it's something good. A lot of them have written about it, and they've talked about it, and they've thought about it a lot. **You see them for an hour, and you're sold.** What you *don't* see is the hundreds or thousands of hours that they've been thinking and planning and sharpening and fine-tuning their enthusiasm and their presentation.

This is something that you can learn to do. Don't think that you can't.

CHAPTER FIVE

A great salesperson cannot make anyone buy something they don't want... That's why we must get prospects to "<u>raise</u> <u>their</u> <u>hand</u>" and show us that they are interested.

✓ Let the prospects qualify themselves by jumping through the hoops we hold in front of them!

✓ This is the secret to making <u>easy</u> sales!

A Great Salesperson's Biggest Limitation

No matter how good he or she is, a salesperson can't make someone buy something that they don't want. That's why you have to get prospects to do what we call "raising their hand" to show you that they're interested. **Prospects qualify themselves by jumping through some kind of metaphoric hoop.** By taking a series of actions or steps, they prove that they really are serious about the type of thing you're offering. **That's the secret to making easy sales: get them to make some kind of initial response first.**

We use direct mail for that, but you can also use space advertising or any other types of media, including TV or radio. **The idea is to get people to buy a low cost offer or respond to a free offer that forces them to take some steps:** to call a phone number, listen to a recorded message, send for an audio CD or DVD, whatever it takes to make that initial sale to them. We've got a promotion right now that we're just getting ready to test, and it's a brand new area for us. We're asking for anywhere from $1,000 to $10,000 for the ultimate sale we're trying to make, and yet we know the best way to get somebody to buy is to start with a prequalified prospect. **You usually can't take somebody from cold to hot immediately, in one step; it's a process.**

In the first offer we're testing here, we're asking for $39 for a discovery package where we lay out the basic ideas in this $1,000- $10,000 offer we're ultimately going to make. Now, will that $39 offer get us the kind of pre-qualified prospective buyer we need to then turn around and give us that $1,000- $10,000? We don't know yet. It might turn out, after we do some testing, that we'll need to use a $19 or $9 offer. We might find that by lowering the price, we open up the funnel, so to speak: we have more people going through the top of the funnel who will come out the bottom paying us that $1,000-$10,000. Or, we could find out the exact opposite. Instead of $39, we may have to charge $49 or $59 or $99 to qualify our prospects.

It's all done through testing here, but the principal remains the same. **You've got to prequalify. You've got to do things to get people to raise their hands.** Actions do speak louder than words. Anybody can *say* that they're interested, but it's by the actions that they take that they prove that they really, truly are. Look at how other people are doing such things. **Get on the other side of the cash register, and start responding to different people's two-step offers, and see how they handle it.** Save the materials they send you. Don't hide from their salespeople when they call you on the phone. Listen to their sales presentations. Learn from them.

With something like this, you're trying to get people to take a small set of actions that lead to a much larger set of actions that you want them to take. You've got to get the right message to the right person in the right way. In that equation, **the most important variable is *the right person*,** because that's where all the money you want to make has to come from. This is true whether you're selling in print, or online, or face-to-face, or on the phone. I know this concept sounds simple, but I'm surprised at how many people have never really thought this through. The idea is to get people to show they're interested first, because you usually can't make someone buy something they don't want. That's a universal truth: people are not buying with guns to their heads. Now, you *can* force someone to do something under duress, and certainly that happens. But in the normal world of commerce, people buy or don't buy at will.

That's the first thing you need to remember here. No matter how good a salesperson you are, there's no magic trick that will pull someone's wallet out and get them to pay for something they haven't chosen to pay for. When you start with that understanding, you realize that you have to figure out how to find the people who *want* to buy what you're selling. **Your first step is to find the right marketplace.** There are more than 307 million people in the U.S. right now, representing a huge number of markets and micro-markets consisting of individuals who like and dislike all kinds of things. The marketplace we happen to serve the most often here at M.O.R.E., Inc. is the business opportunity market. **That's a marketplace of people who are interested in business opportunities that allow them to stay home and make extra money.**

There are different subsets within this marketplace. On one end, there are people who will stop at nothing to make millions of dollars; on the other, there are people who are just looking for a little bit of a retirement supplement. They'd be happy with a few thousand dollars a month. And, naturally, there are many people who fall in between those extremes. Let's say they're in their 40s or 50s, and they're looking for a nest egg to build their retirement account—a steady income that can allow them to invest money for their golden years, 20 or 30 years down the road.

Clearly this is a broad marketplace, made up of all kinds of people. **But still, according to most estimates, there are only a few million people—10 or 15 million at most—who are looking for a business opportunity of some kind.** So: what do you do to try to identify the people who will be interested what you have to offer? **You craft offers that get people to raise their hands and** *say* **that they're interested.** They identify themselves. Now, they don't have to say they're interested in exactly what you have, but they do have to be interested in the general category of products. **That's part of the lead generation process.** Not only do we get people to raise their hand at a specific offer we've made, we also know that people "raise their hands" by buying other products and services offered by other people in our marketplace.

That means we can rent mailing lists of people that have bought business opportunities from other marketers, which lets us identify people within the broad marketplace who are looking for the kinds of products and services we sell. More directly, we could run an ad in a big national newspaper like *USA Today*, which reaches millions of people, many of whom aren't interested in business opportunities. We could use that ad to get prospects to identify themselves by calling a toll-free hotline or visiting a website and raise their hands that way. **So basically, you start with a broad market, and then you do things to determine which people are most likely to want what you sell.**

Again, you can only get someone to buy something you offer because they choose to buy it themselves. They make that decision on their own, but it starts with a hand raiser—with getting people to take the first step and identify themselves as a prospect. **You can only reach someone with a sales message that *wants* to be reached with that sales message.**

That doesn't mean that a particular individual isn't interested in what you're selling; **they've just made it clear that they don't want to be reached by standard marketing methods for one reason or another.** Let's say I'm a closet chocolate lover. Every time I go to the store, I pay cash for chocolate, so there's no trail. I always have a big stash of it at my house... but I've never told anybody that I like chocolate, so I'm never going to be a part of the chocolate marketplace. I've never made myself available to any list, and I've never raised my hand and identified my interest. Therefore, I'm virtually undetected: I fly under the radar screen in the chocolate world. If someone was testing the world's greatest chocolate bar, they would never send me a promotion to try, because I've never identified myself as being a member of that marketplace.

It's the same thing with any marketplace. **Until someone identifies themselves as having interest, they remain under the radar and outside the influence of the people targeting that marketplace.** Oh, I could see an ad on TV advertising a product and I could go pick one up that way. So this concept isn't entirely without flaws, but you get my point. **In a marketing sense, you market to people who have identified themselves as being interested in what you have to offer. That's how you reach a targeted marketplace.**

STEALTH MARKETING!

So you have to figure out first how to get your prospects to raise their hands and show you they're interested in what you have to offer. Then, once you've identified them, you ask them to make a purchase. You're showing them all the benefits they're going to receive when they make their purchase, and trying to influence them that way; but in the end, it's up to them. **You identify the marketplace, you ask them to make a purchase, and if everything goes right—if your marketing system is working smoothly and correctly—you have money flowing into your business as you get people to respond to your offers.**

CHAPTER SIX

❧Fail forward!❧

Q. What's the secret of success?

A. Making great decisions.

Q. What's the secret to making great decisions?

A. Make as many bad decisions as you can — as quickly as you can — and learn from them!

Fail Forward

What's the secret of success? Basically, it's to make great decisions and then implement them correctly. **The secret to making great decisions is to make as many _bad_ decisions as you can, as quickly as you can, and then learn from them.** There's so much to say here, because when we're talking about making bad decisions, we're talking about adversity, struggles, setbacks, problems, challenges, stress, and probably some other great synonyms. These are things that nobody really wants in their life (except the occasional freak). Only an abnormal person would say, "Bring it on, baby. Give me more pain. Give me more problems." **And yet, to truly succeed, you have to learn what it's like to fail.**

As Ben Franklin once pointed out, **"Whatever is painful is also instructive."** I like that quote because, frankly, all of my most important lessons were learned the hard way. I'm sure it's the same for you. When times are good, I don't learn much. **I enjoy those times, but the real lessons come from the hard times, the painful times, the challenges.**

As a general rule, the more money you want to make, the more problems you're going to have... and you know, people just don't want to hear that. Hey, _I_ don't want to hear it either! **But if you want to make millions of dollars, you have to also be willing to accept a millions of dollars worth of**

headaches. Everybody wants the money; nobody wants the headaches. Everybody wants the benefit; nobody wants to do the work it takes to get that benefit. In business, all that work means struggle, adversity, setbacks, challenges. Those are where your best lessons come from, and it's not easy.

But first of all: if it *was* easy, everybody would be doing it. And they're not. According to the last statistics I've read, only 2% of the U.S. population makes over $80,000 a year, which is pretty sad to me, because it's not that difficult to make $80,000 a year. But again, if it was easy, everybody would be doing it. We know they're not. **And then, number two—and this is kind of odd, but there's some truth to it—if everybody *was* rich, nobody would *want* to be rich.** Part of the reason that people aspire to big goals is because they're hard to accomplish. Some people do this for egotistical reasons, so they can feel they're superior to others. Some of it is just because it's difficult. **There's a part of us that likes things to be a little difficult, whether we want to admit it or not.** It's those things in life that we pay the highest prices for, both in our personal lives and in business, that we tend to value the most. The things we pay the least for we tend to discount. That's one of the reasons why there are so many talented people who take their own talents for granted, and a lot of spoiled people who never count their blessings because everything came too easily for them.

So when it comes to business, it's all about struggle. It's all about adversity. **It's all about learning what you have to learn and putting it into play.** And most of the time, the only way to do that is by going through a lot of hell, because that's how you gain experience. **You make a lot of bad decisions and**

learn from them; eventually, you learn enough that you don't go through all that again.

I've known some very smart people in my life, including my step-dad, Don. I remember having so many conversations with Don; he was a really smart guy, and he wouldn't argue back with me. He would just sort of smile a little when I was trying to argue with him; basically, what he was saying to me was, "You'll see. You'll find out." He knew that I still had a lot of learning to do, even though I thought I knew it all. He was too smart to argue with me... but the smile on his face basically said it all.

That was the smile of experience. I run into entrepreneurs like that all the time. They've been out there at war for decades, and they just know things. They've learned those things the hard way, by going through the pain that you have to be willing to go through to succeed. **That doesn't mean you _will_ go through all of it; you just have to be willing to do so. Be willing to do whatever it takes.** And part of what it takes, of course, is bulling right through the tough times. It doesn't feel good; in fact, it can feel very bad sometimes. You want to give up; you want to quit; you want things to be easier. And yet you have to go through what you go through, and you learn as you go along, and get better and smarter. That's how you learn your best lessons. That's how you become wise.

So I want you to just think about that. **The only real failure is giving up—when you just quit trying, or you're really not going for it anymore.** You give up your dreams, and you're just sort of coasting. You can do that occasionally, and you should, just to avoid getting totally burned out. You can coast for brief periods—but otherwise, you should always be reaching for something. **You should always be trying to learn.**

And think on paper. Sometimes, when things get especially challenging for you, just start trying to map out the things you've learned, the different things you've gone through. Sometimes, through the process of writing it all out and looking at it on paper, you'll see solutions that you didn't see before. And also, you'll see that although there may be 10 things wrong in your life, there may also be 10 things right. **You'll weigh things out and see that things aren't always as bad as you think they might be.**

A lot of failing forward in the direct response marketing business involves testing, where you're trying a lot of different ideas, finding what works the best, and then trying to roll that out. You take the ideas that have worked well in your marketplace, and see how many ways you can expand on those ideas, how many different ways you can use variations of those ideas. Think of every test that doesn't work out as failing forward. You're trying a new idea. If it doesn't work, learn from that. You'll have a few winners, and you'll have a whole lot of losers. **But as long as you're learning something from each one of those losers, and you're continuing to tweak the process, you haven't failed.**

Ultimately, the concept is simple. You can lose money on nine out of 10 of your tests and still win. You can fall flat on your face, and as long as you're testing small and not putting a whole lot of money into those tests, you don't lose everything. Let's say you spend $1,000 each on 10 different things. That's $10,000; but those all represent little tests. Nine of them fail, so you just lost nine grand... but let's say the 10th idea was the one that really worked, and it made you your $10,000 back and then some. Well, then, you know people like the idea—so you could roll it out in a big way, and potentially make hundreds of thousands or millions of dollars on it. I know this works, because I've done it plenty of times! **You can lose money on nine out of 10 ideas and still succeed financially.** You can even lose money on 99 out of 100 ideas, as long as you find the one winner in the large group of losers, and you're able to roll out that winner in a big way. **That's what this whole failing-forward concept is all about.**

Now, don't be intimidated by all these super-successful entrepreneurs out there, the ones who are extremely confident and rolling in the dough. They're doing things this exact way. If you study the history of one of these people, you're probably going to discover that unless they were born with a silver spoon in their mouth (and sometimes even then), they've gone through a tremendous amount of pain, challenges, and all kinds of difficulty. **They've gone through hell, and they've learned what they had to learn.** They've paid the price... and that's the same thing that you're going to have to do.

I'm rereading a biography of Ted Turner that was written in the late 1990s, and it's a great book. Everybody knows that the guy became a multi-billionaire, but what they *don't* see is all the pain and the difficulties that he had to go through to get there. And it's not just him; this is true of all highly successful entrepreneurs. They continue to fail forward. **They've had all kinds of things that just didn't work, and they had to keep their enthusiasm up there all the time, and they had to keep**

trying new ideas.

That's failing forward. **I think this is a concept that's lost on a lot of people, because we don't really think about success through failure.** That concept doesn't compute. We think of success as being this thing that just happens, or that somehow you either have it or you don't have it, that there's no journey to it or that it's not a lifelong process of discovery. **Well, success *is* a journey, and part of that journey to success is failing forward.** The secret of success, as it's defined in this particular point, is making great decisions—and how do you make great decisions? By making as many bad ones as possible on your way to discovering the good ones.

Think of a photographer. There are photographers who certainly have an eye toward creativity; they're artists, and they can see shots that other people can't. They know what angles to use, and they know that the lighting needs to be right. **But beyond all of those things that can be learned, a lot of it just boils down to taking a lot of pictures.** Now, we live in a digital world today. You can just delete the photos you don't like, and you're left with the good ones. It wasn't always that way. Back in the days of 35-millimeter film, I remember taking pictures and then going and getting them developed and anticipating. If you go back far enough—and it wasn't that long ago, really— there was no one-hour photo; you had to wait a while for your photos to be developed. I remember fondly the anticipation of getting a roll of film, and waiting to see if I had any good ones in there. Sometimes the whole roll was crap: I didn't take a single good picture, especially when I was a kid. Sometimes I'd look at the pictures and say, "What was I thinking?"

Well, it used to be that way even with professionals. They would have to take a lot of photos, and they would develop their film in their darkroom, and then they would have to go through and figure out which ones were good or bad. Nowadays, that's so much easier to do that than it used to be! You just look at them on a computer, and delete the ones that are bad. In some cases that allows you to be a better photographer, even if you're an amateur, because you know you can just click, click, click, taking hundreds of photos and deleting the bad ones. You don't have to pay to get all the bad ones developed like you used to. **That's sort of the concept of achieving success. It's like a photographer snapping a bunch of pictures.**

When you're talking about failing your way forward to success, you're talking about achieving a lot of results, and no, not all of those results are going to be good. When you run a direct-mail campaign, and you put a promotion in the mail and anticipate the response, sometimes that response is what you're looking for and sometimes it isn't. And the degrees of success vary greatly from promotion to promotion. You might have one that does okay and makes a profit, but it's not the kind of profit you were looking for; yet that minimal success will also help you fail forward.

I've talked before about taking massive action, and I think that strategy applies here also. **The actions you take will determine your level of success.** Someone who dabbles in business or just does a little bit here and there every once in a while isn't likely to see a lot of success, because they're not real serious. They do something every once in a while; they run an ad, maybe, or they do something on the Internet. They are trying to be a player in social media. They're on Facebook and Twitter, but they only log in once a month. They post very sporadically. That may achieve a certain level of success—a certain *low* level of success. You're not going to master social media by logging onto your accounts once every month or two. **The way to master online social media, or to master *anything*, is repetition and taking massive action.**

Another analogy that I'll use is the sports world. There's a lot that separates someone who makes it to the major leagues or plays in the NFL versus someone who plays in the Peewee leagues. Both of them understand the game, but **what makes the difference is commitment.** Let's take baseball and the World Series as an example. A person playing on a World Series team understands the basic game of baseball. A person who plays on a junior high team *also* understands the basic game of baseball. They both know what you're supposed to do with the bat. They know what you're supposed to do with the ball. They know where the bases go. They probably both understand the rules. Now, it's possible that someone playing in the World Series understands the rules of baseball a little bit better than a junior high kid—but probably not much, because the important rules aren't that hard to grasp.

But why are there so few Major League baseball players? Why are there many, many people making up all the levels underneath them—the independent leagues, the minor leagues, and all that? **Some of it's luck, but most of it is the ability to take massive action toward their success.** If they want to play on a team that makes it to the World Series, some of that is out of their control; but if they at least want to play in the Major

Leagues, they have to be dedicated to their craft. **They practice all the time—and they fail a lot.** Baseball players strike out constantly; even the best players, the ones who make millions of dollars, don't get on base every time. Often, their batting average is only around two to three base hits per every 10 at-bats. They call it batting 200 or 300. The hits don't happen very often; more often than not, they strike out or they pop out. But they're constantly doing things to practice and to improve their game... even as the pitchers, catchers, and fielders are doing all they can to improve theirs.

To bring it back to business: **the level of success you achieve in the end is directly related to how many times you tried and failed during the process.** Now, of course, the goal is to learn something from those failures. **You can do something wrong over and over again and you're never going to get it right unless you're learning from the mistakes you've made.** You can't forget to learn from them! True success comes from learning them as quickly as possible. Take massive action, fail forward, and make as many mistakes as need to, as long as you're *learning* from those mistakes and as long as you're always moving forward. Now, you never know how long this is going to take. **Sometimes breakthroughs happen quickly, and sometimes they take a long time.** But success *will* happen as long as you're learning from your mistakes and you're using this concept of failing forward.

Let me re-emphasize that this process can be emotionally painful at times. It can feel like you're weighed down, in a fog, not knowing where you're going or how you're going to get there. **Part of the trick of working through this is to**

recognize the supreme value in persevering, as long as you're learning and moving forward. Remind yourself that this too will pass. It's a necessary part of the process of gaining the knowledge, skills and experience you need.

Here's a true-life example of that, and I've mentioned it before on other Ways. The first time I ever saw a sales letter being written by a capable, competent copywriter was when we hired Russ Von Hoelscher to be our consultant. He would come out to our house back in 1989, when we were just six months into our direct response business. Before that, we had hired a freelance copywriter to write our first sales letter. Although I tweaked it and played with it, I had never written one from scratch myself.

So Russ came out to the house, and I watched him write several sales letters. We would drink coffee and brainstorm, then all of a sudden, Russ would get an idea and he'd just start writing frantically. Eileen and I would shut up while Russ did that. Eventually he'd run out of steam, and we'd drink some more coffee. We'd talk a little more about the particular product or service that he was helping us to develop; then he'd do it again. When he left, we'd take all these legal pads that he'd written copy on to our typist, she would type them up, and we would send these letters out to our customers. Then the customers would send in their money.

I got a chance to see a capable, competent, experienced direct response copywriter develop these sales letters from start to finish, letters that were then translated into cold hard cash. I got so excited about this that I decided I had to learn how to do that myself—I just had to! So I started working on it, and it took me eight years of hard work to become a good enough copywriter to develop a sales letter that actually produced profits from an outside mailing list of people that didn't know us—people with whom no previous relationship had been established. **During those eight years, I wrote many sales letters that actually produced revenue from our own existing customer list, people we had a relationship with.** But whenever I tried to take an offer outside of our customer base, it flopped. I worked so hard, too. Since that time, we've experienced some major successes—and now I write a lot of my copy with Chris Lakey. Chris has developed these skills as well.

Skills like these are developed over a period of time by, usually, going through some very difficult and challenging situations.

Remember: the things we value the most are the things we pay the highest prices for. That price isn't always money: it also includes the struggle and adversity that we have to go through to get there. **So now, one of the things I'm most proud of is having the ability to put sales letters together that can potentially be very profitable.** Not that they all are; in fact, a good part of testing is being willing to lose money in order to make money.

You succeed by failing first, then trying again. Nobody wants to lose money... and yet losing money is part of the game of business. And if you study the lives of the people that made it in the biggest way, you'll see that not only did they make millions of dollars, they also *lost* millions of dollars too. My best recent story about that involves T. Boone Pickens, a name that's probably familiar to you. At the time we're recording this,

STEALTH MARKETING!

Pickens is probably close to 80 years old. I saw him interviewed on a popular news show about five years ago, and he was making incredible amounts of money—having gone through a financial roller-coaster ride for decades. Well, they asked him when he was going to retire, and he said, **"Look, I'm just now figuring out how to do this."** And he was having the time of his life, working around a bunch of young people. He was really happy. I found out a couple of years later that he had gone through a really tough time and lost almost all of his fortune *again*. But he's probably still out there doing it.

Stories like these can be inspirational, but they can also be instructive. And of course, it's easy to acknowledge the fact that losing money is part of making money, as long as it's not *us* losing money. **But you have to be willing to take that chance, and keep moving forward... and failing forward, whenever you have to.**

CHAPTER SEVEN

Wealth-Builder's Rule #1:

Make damn sure that the bulk of your income is not dependent on the number of actual hours you work. *After all, who makes more money — the brain surgeon or the rock star?*

Wealth Builder's Rule #1

Here's my #1 wealth building rule: make damned sure that the bulk of your income is *not* dependant on the number of hours that you actually work. After all, who makes more money: the brain surgeon, or the rock star? We all know it's the rock star, though in the end, the brain surgeon may actually do better—because they might do a better job of investing their money, instead of blowing it like a lot of these rock stars do. But let's look at how these two people make their money.

The rock star makes money on the sales of albums, CDs and DVDs, and they do concerts where they might pull 80,000 people into a stadium. If they're getting a piece of the gate, they're making a fortune. Now, while some of that is dependent on the number of hours they work, a lot of it isn't. The same is true of bestselling authors: they might write one book and make millions. And look at movie stars. Jack Nicholson was reportedly paid $50 million and got producer credits to work for 10 days in his role in the 1992 movie *A Few Good Men*. He was paid on things other than the number of hours that he worked. By then, he'd built such a reputation that any movie with him in it was sure to increase the likelihood that the movie would be profitable, too.

In our business, as in any business, there are things that you can do to make huge sums of money regardless of the number of hours you put in. **You're working smart, not just working hard.** You're working *on* your business, as well as *in* your business. **You're doing things like planning, dreaming, and scheming, coming up with all kinds of ideas for products and services that you can sell to your customers—and then to people you've never done business with.** This all involves trying to think through your business from a structural point of view.

I've mentioned that I'm rereading a book on Ted Turner right now. Turner is an amazing entrepreneur, for several reasons. Among other things, he's great at working *on* his business, not *in* his business. **And he's great at making connections and understanding the overall concepts of how all the different things that he's involved with tie together.** But throughout his entire career, his critics have laughed at him—not always behind his back, either. Some of them have been very vocal about the fact that he overpays for everything, at least according to them. They say, "If you want to sell something, sell it to Ted, because he'll pay way more money than it's worth!" Whatever major business asset that you have—whether it's a TV station, radio station, movie library, whatever it is—if Ted Turner is a good prospective buyer for it, you want to sell it to him, because he overpays for everything.

That's the running joke; and yes, he does overpay on a lot of these things. But he also has a way of knowing which things are worth overpaying for. **He sees his businesses in a very conceptual way, in that he grasps intuitively how everything connects.** That's why he buys some of the things he overpays for: they tie in with his other business models. Often, he makes something work where it couldn't work otherwise. **All that requires a deep level of thinking.** It's all about looking at your business as if it's an intellectual game, like a chess game where you keep score with money. You really have to put a lot of thought into something like that; and on the face of it, the time that you spend doing that may seem unproductive.

Here's a personal example. **There's a certain thing I often do, especially during times when I'm going through a tough business period.** As soon as I wake up, I walk upstairs and turn on the shower. While the water is heating up, I run downstairs and pour myself a cup of coffee. I have a shower that I can sit in, so that that's nice. It's got a little seat in it. And five minutes from the time I first woke up, I'm drinking my first cup of coffee, and I'm drinking it under the shower. Of course, I hold the cup out so the water doesn't dilute my coffee—**but I'm drinking a cup of coffee, and I'm running that hot water, and I'll just sit in the shower for 30 minutes sometimes, thinking.**

Well, I think that this morning, I sat in the shower for probably an hour total. I actually did it three different times this morning—just letting the hot water run, just thinking. That's all I'm doing in that situation: I'm just thinking. To some people, it would just look like I was screwing off. "What did you do this morning, TJ?" "Well, I sat in the shower for an hour." They might think I was a lazy bum, but I had a legal pad and pen outside the shower. **After a while, I would towel dry and then sit in my chair and drink more coffee and sketch out ideas and write things down.** In times like that, I don't have all the answers by any means; I'm just trying to think things through.

STEALTH MARKETING!

That's important work.

In one of his books, Napoleon Hill talked about how Henry Ford had an efficiency expert come in to tell him how to run his business more efficiently. After the very first day, the guy said, "Well, Mr. Ford, I'm still working on all the angles, but I can tell you one thing for sure. You know that guy about five offices down?" He mentioned the guy's name, and then said, "You need to get rid of him." And Ford said, "Yeah? Why is that?" And the expert said, "I walked by his office a number of times today, and he always had his feet up on the desk. I'd swear he was sleeping."

And then Henry Ford laughed and told him that particular guy had invented and helped implement a number of ideas that, in the past year, had earned the Ford Motor Company millions of dollars. **You see, it may have looked on the surface like he was sleeping, but he was really just thinking.** He had his eyes closed, he had his feet up on the desk, and he was thinking deeply. It's important to think that way. **If you're skilled at it, if you develop the ability to really understand your business at an intimate level, then you can see how everything connects conceptually.** Any time that you spend just dreaming about different products, services or offers that would work well for your customers and the markets that you serve is time well spent. Again, you're not getting paid by the hour, necessarily. **You are getting paid by the quality of the ideas that you come up with, and how you then implement those ideas.**

Also: the smartest, most successful people in this world don't try to do everything themselves. They try to work through a small team of other people to implement their ideas. In building this cadre, they're trying to find people who are very talented—in many cases people who are smarter than they are in specific fields, and who have all kinds of skills and abilities that they don't. **They harness other people's skills and talents to the advantage of all involved.** If this method is coupled with what I've talked about here previously, it will produce revenue from your market. That's all time well spent; that's working smart, not working hard.

Later today, I'm going to meet with Chris Lakey, Shelley Webster, and Drew Hansen. Shelly is our general manager, Chris is the Marketing Director for all of our companies, and Drew Hansen is our Vice President in charge of Customer Relations. The four of us are going to be brainstorming. We're going to spend an hour just mapping out different ideas for the End of the Year promotion that we do every year. **That's going to be an hour very well spent—because not only will it contain the best of all the thinking that I've been doing lately, it will also tap into the minds of three other very smart people who intimately understand our business.**

All business clichés aside, there *is* such a thing as working smart, not just working hard. **This can include anything that you do to enhance the value of your mailing list, or anything you're doing to find better suppliers—often things that don't spring to mind right away.** I spent a lot of time this past weekend investigating suppliers on the Internet, trying to find unique deals and other unusual things. If you find the right combination of factors when doing things like this, you can make (or save) an awful lot of money. Seen from the outside, it might not seem like you're really working—but you are.

STEALTH MARKETING!

The worst mistake someone can make is to somehow equate the amount of money you make with how hard you work, or to think that if you work harder or spend more hours doing something, that somehow translates to making more money. Many times this is not true, which is why we have a big class warfare problem in American politics. That's why politicians are always pitting the working class against the CEOs and other people who get paid huge amounts of money. These people are often compensated not for the hours they work, and not even necessarily by wages. They get paid bonuses and stock options and royalties, and their investments are all paying off; they're getting paid for past work. But we've got this general distaste for people whose income doesn't come from the amount of time they put in. And that's really the result of faulty thinking, which is what brings us to Wealth Building Rule #1.

Again, the bulk of your income should come from things aside from the actual time you put in at work. I used the example of the brain surgeon and the rock star; but there are also many examples in the acting industry. Think of the actor who gets paid a certain mixed amount to make a picture; and then you've got the producer or the writer and other people that are involved at the production level, who not only get paid to make the movie or TV show, but who get paid on the DVD sales and all the other business that comes along with it—the merchandising and all these other revenue streams.

And in some cases, when you look at movies specifically, once they're out of the theatre they actually make more money than they did initially. So it's a steal for them to pay an actor several million dollars to make the movie, because they know that their payday is going to come later. They're going to reap huge dividends as the movie makes it way to DVDs, into Netflix and iTunes and all the other distribution channels. If it's wildly successful, hey, McDonald's is giving away the toys in their Happy Meals, and there's even more money. **You've got other merchandise tie-ins that bring them even more revenue. All those things happen *independently* of the number of hours that they put in actually making the movie.**

That's what you have to do to really rake in the cash. **Put yourself in a position where you've got revenue coming in, regardless of the time you put into something.** That doesn't mean you're going to put in just a little bit of time; it doesn't mean that you're lazy; it doesn't mean you sit around and do nothing all day. **However, it *does* mean that the way you handle your day is different from someone who's paid directly for the time they put in.** Consider someone who works in a factory: they're paid only when they're clocked in. They drive to the office or to the factory, they punch their time card, and they immediately go to work making widgets.

They make widgets all day until lunchtime, and then they clock out for that. Later they go back to work until the end of their day and they punch out, and they're done making widgets for a while. They go home and don't think about it until the next day, when they go back, punch in, and do the same thing over again. Occasionally they get vacations and holidays, and other time off for various things. At the end of the year they've put in X number of hours, and they know they get paid X dollars per hour and it's easy to do the math, and that's it.

For someone who gets paid for their ideas, or who turns

their ideas into cash independently of the amount of time they work, the day might look differently. **Most people would never have the time to take an hour-long shower, as I did this morning.** Most people are in a hurry to get to the office, or to get to the job. They get up as late as possible, because they need their sleep, because they stayed up late the night before. They rush around and grab breakfast, take a quick shower and are in the car. Maybe they have time to grab a Starbucks or something on the way, but that's it, because they need to get to the office and clock in as quickly as possible, because they're not paid until they do.

I can take an hour-long shower because when you get down to it, I'm working when I do that. I'm thinking about business and working on ideas in my head; and some other time during the day, I might walk outside and shoot some baskets, or go play with the dog, or do some other thing where I'm not really thinking about the office or worrying about work-related things. I go back to work a little bit later.

Now, I happen to be a morning person; but say I was like my friend and colleague Alan Bechtold, who happens to be a night owl. He's up late at night doing those things, because that's when he works best. **My point is, your day is not dependent on a specific, set range of time; it's not even dependant on being in the office, necessarily.** Sometimes, when you're following this principle, your day may be spent at the beach or on a golf course, and you can still be working. Your work isn't dependent on a specific set of actions—unlike, say, a surgeon, who has to spend his day cutting people open. A lot of your day is spent dreaming; not in the sense that you're wasting time or wishing you had more money, but in the sense that you're working in a mental world, thinking through business and spending time planning and preparing for what's coming next.

One of the nice things about entrepreneurship is that once you get involved in a business, and you start dreaming in this way, you never really stop. Your brain is constantly working on business; so even in your recreational times or rest periods, it's always in the back of your mind. You never know where an idea is going to come from. I often get them in the shower like I did this morning. You could be on vacation, or driving down the road, or sitting in your office when the concept strikes. Your brain is working the same, no matter which situation you're in. **In fact, sometimes the best ideas happen when you're not really planning on them.** You might get a breakthrough idea because of something you read in the newspaper or saw on TV; maybe a commercial or sitcom triggered a thought, and that idea turned into something you jotted down; and maybe later, that note turned into a sales letter that turned into money.

Some days, I sit there in front of the computer screen and I might play around with just one page of sales copy. I'm just fiddling with ideas; I may not look like I'm doing much, but I'm exercising a lot of brain cells. **There's a lot of thinking happening during days like those, and hopefully the next day is when it gets turned into something that you can actually see.** It's hard to quantify mental labor. When you produce widgets, it's simple enough to say, "Well, today I produced a 100 widgets." But how do you quantify hours spend in the realm of thoughts and ideas, and the mental convolutions necessary to turn those ideas into a product, or into a service, or into an offer, or a website, or anything that then becomes a part of your business model?

What you achieve through thought isn't necessarily dependent on the number of hours you work. **It's more about the energy you put into it, and the thinking that comes out as you do your business—not so much the actual hours you put in.** In many ways, it's hard to discuss this, **because it's all very conceptual. The main thing to consider here is that when you're in business for yourself, you never really stop working.** Sure, you always put in a lot of hours; but it's a different kind of productivity than when you're working for somebody else.

The most successful people in the world are *not* getting paid by the hour. Being an entrepreneur gives you all kinds of potentials to work not just harder but smarter: to work through other people, and leverage yourself and your assets. **That's really what all this is about: it all boils down to forms of leverage.**

CHAPTER EIGHT

The "4-M's" to create your own money-machine:

→ MODELS — Why create, when you can steal? What works for one will work for you. There are plenty of proven models you can steal from. Do it!

→ MARKETING — Attracting prospects and customers! Selling, re-selling, and re-selling again and again!

→ MARGINS — Make your promotions fail-proof... even with low response rates! Make your margins high! Higher! Highest!

→ MANAGEMENT — Organizing, systematizing, controlling, auto-pilot, absentee ownership mentality.

The Four M's

This chapter covers what I call the four M's of creating your own money machine. You see, that's what most people really want: a money machine, not a business *per se*. All they really want are the benefits that a business provides. **In order to accomplish that for yourself, you have to set these four things in place: Models, Marketing, Margins, and Management.** These are the basics of any business. Think about them as the four cylinders of an engine; if all four are working properly, that engine runs smoothly, pumping out copious amounts of a fifth M: Money.

Let's consider the concept of Models first. Here's what I think you should remember most when it comes to Models: why create something new, when you can borrow bits and pieces of what's working for other people? Anything that's working for others, or even what's worked for *you* in the past, can be re-tweaked and turned into something workable today. There are plenty of proven models that you can steal from. **These models are roadmaps, formulas, shortcuts—instant answers on the path to monetary success. Just find somebody else who's making a lot of money, and adapt some of the things they're doing to your own business.**

Needless to say, **I'm not talking about plagiarism;** you should never just take someone else's work. But there *are* many models out there that you can adapt to your business, and let's face it: there's very little that's truly innovative. Oh, you occasionally see someone try something utterly new... but often, that very newness makes it unfamiliar, and dooms it to failure. **It's better to find something that's already proven, and then modify it a little.** If you can model your promotions after existing successful promotions in your marketplace, then you can be at least somewhat confident in the results that you'll receive. The company you're modeling yourself after has already done what you're trying to do; so if you present a similar promotion with a slightly different feel, you may be able to capitalize on their model. **You can expect a better chance of success, assuming you're offering a good product and can deliver on the benefits you're promising.** So take advantage of this concept.

You can look for models everywhere. A model might be as simple as the way a website looks, and the kinds of elements you can incorporate into your own site, if you're selling online. It could involve modeling a mail piece, where you're instituting a specific technique that others are using that seems to be attracting buyers. Maybe it's a hook, a kind of angle they're taking with their marketing. **The point is, find models that are working. This is a good reason to keep a swipe file.**

Here's what I mean by that: just keep a file of other people's successful promotions, things that you know have worked for them, and put those ideas into play in your own promotions. This is especially helpful if you're trying to get something done quickly. **And keep this in mind: as long as you're borrowing a little here and a little there from a lot of sources, you're not really stealing anything.** Ideas can't be copyrighted anyway. You're just taking concepts that are working for others and putting them together in a unique way.

This is a great way to solve a lot of the confusion and frustration inherent in business. Just look for as many models as you can; get on the other side of the cash register, try to determine what it is about those ideas that are working well for other people, and implement them in your own promotions. **Learn to recognize good sales copy, and then learn to write that way yourself.**

Once you do a few promotions of your own, you can model after yourself. If a specific promotion worked well for you, then adapt the best elements of it for the next one. You might make the envelope look the same, or make the text the same color, or go with a very similar order form. This kind of modeling can help you get things done much, much faster.

The next M, Marketing, is all the things you do to attract and retain customers, and *this* **is where you need to spend the majority of your time.** Earlier, I discussed the hour I spent in the shower one recent morning. That was composed of several trips; when I'd run out of ideas, I'd go right back in the shower. I'd sit under that hot water, drink some coffee, and get my brain all nice and caffeinated. Well, when I do that, I'm marketing. I'm thinking about selling and reselling. I'm trying to create irresistible offers that I know our customers will go crazy over—offers so good they won't be able to resist. Anytime you think about all that, you develop your skills, your abilities to become a good marketer. That's where you're making the largest contribution to your business. **That's where you're creating your own money machine, so make sure you excel at marketing—and never delegate it to other people!** Do *not* hire an agency to take of your advertising for you. Learn how to be a good marketer yourself if you really want to make money in this business.

Next up is Margins. Try to come up with as many proprietary products and services as you can: things that have high perceived value, high profit margins, and low development costs. **These are items that are worth a lot of money to your customers, but don't cost a lot of money to reproduce. Proprietary information products are good examples.** Look for high ticket items, where you can make a lot of money even if you get a low response rate. That way, you can make big money with bad numbers. **You have to keep the margins high.** Don't always just be the cheapest date; that will backfire on you. I can honestly tell you that in all the years we've been in business, with the hundreds of different promotions we've offered to our customers over the years, we've lost money only on the low-ticket items. Admittedly, there have been times when we didn't make a lot of money on big-ticket items, but otherwise, **we've never lost money, ever, except when we've sold low-ticket items that didn't have extended back-end upsells attached.** So watch your margins. Anybody can undercut the price; anybody can sell stuff cheap.

You have to be very careful about what you do out there. **Ideally, promotions must be fail-proof even with lower response rates; that's why we sell so many high-ticket items.** If you're in an industry that can't adapt to high-ticket items, then you either need to get into a more amenable industry, or figure out new ways that you can introduce the high-ticket concept to that market. For example, you might consider packaging products together to try to drive your ticket price higher.

Now, don't confuse selling expensive items with having high profit margins; those can be two different things. If you sell a $5,000 package and it cost you $4,500 to fulfill it, well, that's not a very high profit margin. What you need is a $5,000 product that costs you $500 to fulfill, leaving you a hefty $4,500 profit. *That's* a high margin. **So watch your margins, and make sure you have lots of profit built in.** You're never going to be able to anticipate all the costs that you can incur doing business, and you have to account for things like advertising, paying taxes, paying employees, shipping, or paying people to build your widgets for you. Those are all things that eat into your profit margins; and the higher the profit margin, the more easily you can absorb those expenses and leave yourself with a nice profit that you get to keep when all is said and done.

A big part of how you achieve that is through the last M: Management. You need to have competent people, systems, and processes in place so that you can run your business on autopilot. And as far as Management goes, most people don't understand the value of a good management team. Are some managers overpaid? Probably. **And yet, it's the people at the very top of the company who shape the company. Bad management leads to broken money machines, no buts about it.**

Here's an example: there's a company that buys up failed resort properties and hotels so they can turn those properties around and sell them. The first thing the new company does is fire the management—all of them. The reasoning is that if those people were any good at their jobs, the resort wouldn't be struggling in the first place. **Your management team is your brain trust... and if it's flawed, your money machine isn't going to work right. You *have* to surround yourself with the best and the brightest.** That's the secret of my success: to hire people who are talented in areas where I'm not. It's the synergy of a group of people at the top that makes all the difference in the world. A good management team makes life easier for you.

Even if you're a one-man band, even if you're doing it all yourself, you can implement management processes to help. That can mean outsourcing, or turning to a specific company that does all your fulfillments. It might be someone who manages your mailings, which usually means working with a good printer and a good mailing house. **Management *processes* are just as important as management *people*.**

When management is done right, it can keep your money machine well-oiled and working smoothly. It can keep your margins high, it can keep your marketing rolling, and your models will work better because you have good management overseeing your people and processes. **For most people, good management usually means not doing everything yourself.** Even an entrepreneur who works out of his home probably has an accountant managing the paperwork associated with their taxes.

So there are your four M's: Models, Marketing, Margins, and Management. When these things are meshing properly and clicking right along, they can turn your business into a money machine. **Organization is important to an effective marketing system, and those four M's can really set the tone for your success.** So memorize them, and use them on a daily basis. These are proven methods; so don't try to go at it alone. **The formulas are out there. Take them in hand, combine them in the right way, tweak and tune, and soon that money machine will be humming away.**

? ? ? ? ?
Why Direct Mail?

✓ Direct mail can give you tremendous leverage.

✓ Every direct marketing piece is a salesman in an envelope!

✓ It's out there working for you — and making huge numbers of sales, without your direct effort!

✓ Sending out 1,000 direct mail letters is like sending out a sales force of 1,000 of the best salespeople!

Why Use Direct Mail?

This one's a biggie, so I'm going to spend quite a few pages on it. **This one secret, I believe, has made us more money than everything else that we've ever done combined—and then some.** As of this writing, direct mail has been our primary marketing vehicle now for about 23 years. It's made us tens of millions of dollars, and it can make *you* millions of dollars, too. That's the carrot here; that's the thing you need to get really excited about! The potential is unlimited, and all the money you want is just waiting there for you to tap into—just as we and thousands of other companies have done. **Direct mail is worth literally billions of dollars per year!**

Now, the danger here is that you've heard all this before. This may be something that you think you already know about— and yet I challenge you to pay close attention nonetheless. Because if you *really* knew all about direct mail, then you'd already be making millions of dollars with it. If that's not your story—if you're *not* bringing in millions of dollars with this—then maybe you still have some learning to do. And I don't mean that in a cocky, arrogant way; not at all. **Even those who thoroughly understand direct mail are still learning constantly. School is never out for the pro.** Nobody knows it all, and never let anybody ever try to fool you into thinking that they do.

Now, many people call direct mail "junk mail." We beg to

differ; we consider it educational. In fact, we collect this stuff. I've probably saved tons of direct mail over the years... and I play with it like a little kid plays in a sandbox, because it's all about money. The next time you start to throw away a piece of "junk mail," stop for a second and realize that it's probably making somebody a lot of cash... or you wouldn't be receiving it over and over. **Next, consider this: properly handled, what works for one person can work for you, too.** Moneymaking ideas are transferable.

So why use direct mail marketing, as compared to all the other forms of marketing? **Because direct mail can give you tremendous leverage in the marketplace.** I've said it before: every direct marketing piece that you send out is like a salesperson in an envelope. It's out there working for you, making sales (potentially huge numbers of sales) without your direct effort. Sending out 1,000 direct mail letters is like sending out a sales force of 1,000 of the best salespeople, because **you can do a complete and thorough job of selling in a direct mail letter.** Now, sometimes you have to be very creative in how you do it, and later on in this chapter we'll talk to you about a new way that Chris and I are developing to give little direct mail packages huge selling power. It's something we call our Modified One Step. I can't wait to tell you about that.

But first of all, let me remind you about our own direct mail success story. We started with small display ads in a national magazine: two tiny sixth-page display ads. Within six months, we had parleyed them into multiple larger space ads. We were bringing in about $16,000 a month, an average of about $500 a day. Then we met Russ von Hoelscher, and he taught us about direct mail. Within nine months we went from $16,000 a month to almost $100, 000 a week. Within five years, we had generated over $10 million in total revenue; within 20 years, well over $100 million.

Direct mail works primarily through the good, old-fashioned U.S. Postal Service, and it can really give you a tremendous leverage, an amazing advantage over other marketing methods. Your direct mail pieces can be out there working for you, making a huge number of sales without you having to be involved at all. **One of the great things about using a sales letter instead of a salesperson is that you never have to deal directly with the rejection.** The reality of any selling situation is that most people say no. You're never going to have the majority of your prospects tell you yes, which means that your average sales person deals with rejection much more than almost anybody else in society.

You know that poor guy who doesn't realize that he's unattractive and smelly, and every woman he asks out tells him no? Well, a salesperson puts that guy to shame when it comes to rejection. Because even though the ugly guy may be rejected at the bar every night, or at least all weekend long, salespeople deal with rejection constantly, day in and day out. Every call is the risk of another no, the risk of another rejection, the risk of rudeness when people tell you they don't want to hear from you or slam the door in your face. This happens all the time to a salesperson, so they have to build up an immunity to being told no in order for them to do their jobs effectively.

When you send out direct mail letters, the rejection takes the form of people looking at your sales letter and

deciding to throw it in away. You don't have to worry about an
envelope getting offended if it gets thrown in the trash or the
recycling bin. It made the delivery, and that's the end of its
responsibility. That's one of the things that makes direct mail
such a great alternative to an actual door-to-door sales force.
When we talk about door-to-door, of course, we're usually
talking about a small market area. That's another thing that
distinguishes direct mail from classic door-knocking
salesmanship. With classic salesmanship, you want to tackle an
entire town and so you have a sales team that fans out all over
the town to talk to people and knock on doors and try to make
sales. **With direct mail, you can have your sales presentation
being made all over the** *country***, in just a few days' time.**

**Here are five reasons why you should consider direct
mail.** I'll run through them quickly, and then go into more detail
on each. **First** of all, it's targeted marketing. **Second,** direct mail
is one-to-one communication. Number **three,** direct mail gives
you total control, without limitations. Number **four,** it's like a
sales rep in an envelope. **Fifth,** you can test new selling ideas —
new ideas for products and services — for dirt-cheap prices.

Let's take a closer look at each of these, starting with the
targeted aspect of direct mail. Even though we're talking a mass
mailing, **in almost every case direct mail is targeted.** You can
customize your sales message to a specific person or market
area, and you can spend all of your money to reach the people
most likely to do business with you. **This gives you more
control than any other form of advertising that we know of.**
You're not just trying everyone and hoping you'll get the right
person; this isn't one of those Publishers Clearing House things,

110

where you're spending millions of dollars to blanket the entire U.S. with a direct mail campaign. No, you're customizing your sales message to a specific person or market area. **You spend all of your money reaching the people who are most likely to do business with you.** You're more in control over your sales message and your advertising, as opposed to other forms of advertising, which are hit-and-miss.

Furthermore, that kind of targeting means that direct mail is more one-on-one than most advertising. Because it's targeted, your sales message can be extremely personal and confidential. **You can communicate directly to your targets in a highly personal way, and no other kind of advertising lets you connect like this.** It's targeted, so it's extremely personal and confidential. It goes right to the person who's meant to receive it. If you've targeted your marketplace right, let's say by mailing to a rented list of people that you know have bought something similar, you can talk to them as if you know that they're interested, because you know what they're buying. **If you write your copy properly, it's almost like you're having a personal conversation with that individual.**

I often talk about the similarities between a salesperson and a sales letter, and one of the closest similarities is this concept of personal, one-on-one communication. **A good direct mail package models a good salesperson.** One of the very basic things you talk about when you're teaching direct response as a marketing method is that you want to write as if you're writing directly to one person. **That means that instead of using words like "we" or "us," words that would indicate that there's a group involved, you use language like "you" and "I."** You're trying to make it seem like you're sitting across the table from them, making a presentation to them face-to-face. No one else is around, no one else is looking, no one else is listening. **It's a private communication.**

Then there's this third concept, of total control with no limits. For example, there are ways that you can give small direct mail packages, even small postcards, huge selling power. I'll talk about that a bit more when I talk about two-step marketing. **The point is, no other form of advertising allows you that level of control.** Other forms of advertising make you conform to their rules and regulations, although of course you still have basic rules and regulations you have to follow with the FTC even with direct mail, as well as various state and federal laws. Otherwise, you really *are* in control.

With direct mail, you have the ability to make your message be exactly what you want it to be. How long should your sales letter be to do a complete job of selling? It could be as long as you like. There are no limitations, other than, possibly, printing guidelines and weight restrictions. You set the format, the text characteristics, the color of the paper, how it's stapled, how you present the order form. That's all up to you. You have total control over what your direct mail piece or pieces look like.

When you run an ad in a magazine or on the Internet, you're sometimes stuck with the parameters they set. If they say your ad has to be this many words or in this font size, you have to work within those parameters. Well, you don't have that with direct mail. Even weight restrictions aren't that big a deal. If you have good numbers and your numbers can support spending the money, you can mail a brick if you want to. **With direct mail**

you're in control of the entire process, so you have as much selling power as you need. If you want to send a short sales letter, you can. If you want a to mail a long sales letter or even a book, you can do that. You can do whatever you want!

And then the fourth thing: it's a sales rep in an envelope. Because you have no limits, much of the job that's normally reserved for a living and breathing sales rep can be done with direct mail. If you've got 10,000 or 100,000 direct mail pieces out there, it's like having 10,000 or 100,000 salespeople. It gives you tremendous leverage if you do it right. Again, as much story as it takes to sell, you've got the space for it. You can educate the customer. You can show them the advantage and disadvantages of your particular offer. **It does a complete job of selling, making your sales presentation for as long as it takes.** When you open a door to a salesperson, they don't just say, "Hi, I've got a bottle of whatever and I want to sell it to you. Here's how much it costs. Do you want to buy it?"

No, usually their presentation takes at least several minutes, and what they usually try to do is get your attention and hold it. If they can, they try to get inside your door so they can sit at your table with you and show you their product, demo it, and hopefully walk away with a sale. It takes time to do that. **In direct mail, you've got the same ability. You've got the space to do it, however long your story takes to unfold.** That's why it's like putting a sales rep inside an envelope.

Now, most people are afraid to make a direct mail presentation that long. They tend to be shocked at the length of the sales letters that we produce; but they're so long because we understand this principle that it sometimes takes a lot of words to make a sale. **The more you tell, the more you sell.** You need the ability to fully unveil your story, to fully explain to someone why they need your product or service, and a direct mail campaign allows you to do that.

And let's look at number five: you can test new selling ideas dirt-cheap, and then roll out the best of the best performers big-time. Direct mail can be expensive, but you can still test very inexpensively, even though it costs more money per person than with a display ad in a magazine. It becomes the ultimate marketing research tool. It's cheap because you can do small mailings, find out what works the best, and then roll it out with your winners.

Now, you have to be real careful not to test *too* small. When the numbers are too small, you should question the results; you're not able to fully gauge whether it was effective or not. It's the same way with polls. Chris Lakey is a political junkie, and he sees a lot of polls. He tells me that they have to get their sample size big enough so that there's no risk that the response was an anomaly. If the pool of people is too small, there might be a problem that skews the results; maybe a few people were having a bad day, so they responded the wrong way. That's going to mess up the results. That's why you need to call at least a thousand people across a broad spectrum so that you get a good sample of the marketplace that you're polling.

It's the same thing in direct mail. **If you mail too few pieces, you risk having the numbers not work out—either positively or negatively.** If you have a situation where the results weren't good, was that because your offer sucked, or because you happened to get a bad sampling from a mailing list, or was there something else that made them respond poorly? On the other hand, maybe you got a really *good* response, and you've put too much faith in this list sampling. For whatever reason, that particular day, a few more people responded one way or another, and that made your percentages go way up. That could kill you if you roll out big, because the positive response made you think too highly of your mail. That's another reason why you've got to test big enough to have a good idea of whether something's going to work or not.

But don't test too big, either. The whole point of testing is to limit your risk while you're trying to figure out if an idea is going to work or not, or if a particular campaign is going to be profitable. You can test small, target a certain group of people that you want to test the offer to, and then once you know that's worked, you can roll that mailing out to a larger group. Maybe it's done in phases, where, say, you start off with a 1,000 people as a test. From there, you decide to mail to 5,000 people. And then if *that* works, you mail to 10,000 people, and then maybe ultimately you mail to 50,000 or 100,000—or a million people if you have the right offer. **So you start small, and through the testing of new ideas, you find out which ones are going to be the best ones.** Those are the ones you roll out to new customers or bigger portions of your existing customers.

The ability to control everything, I think, is what makes direct mail so powerful. You've got more control over everything, from the list you're mailing to the type of offer you make them. You decide exactly how big your offer is, how many pages are included in your sales material, what format it goes out in, and more. **All of these things add up to control; and**

that puts you in a position to more effectively perform your marketing. Lack of control ends up being detrimental to your business, because among other things, you don't know where your profits are coming from. Even if your ad campaign is working, you don't know which *part* of it is working, and you have no idea of the degree that particular elements are working or not. **If you have control of that, and understand where the profits are coming from, you can more quickly identify things that aren't working so that you can modify your plan.**

That's a basic overview of why direct mail is so valuable, and why I recommend that you turn to it for your own promotions. Even if it hasn't worked for you before, I think that you should give it another shot, with all these things in mind. Or maybe you haven't tried it, because snail mail seems like it's so old-school. Nobody mails anymore; everything's done online, right? **Well, think about that: how many emails have you deleted lately without even looking at them?** If you've got some background in direct response marketing and it's all from the reference point of Internet or online marketing, I would encourage you to think again about using direct mail. **We're seeing a lot of people go back to mail who used to be online exclusively,** because they're finding that they can have more impact on their marketplace and make more profits if they stay in touch with their customers through snail mail.

Over the years we've learned a lot about direct mail, and here's a story I'd like to share on the subject. Back in the late 1990s, we were part of this think tank coaching program that was run by a very famous marketer that most people have heard of. My wife Eileen and I were members for about five years, and this was right when the Internet was getting really big. A couple of Internet marketing gurus were part of our group, and they knew that we were mailing millions of direct mail pieces every year. They used to laugh their asses off at us, because we were a couple of hicks from Kansas who were wasting money mailing all these direct mail packages, while they were involved in this high-tech, super-exciting Internet marketing that cost very little. We were part of the old world, and they were part of this exciting new world.

They didn't even have the courtesy to laugh behind our backs. They got right up in our faces, and they thought it was just so funny that here they were getting ahead in the new world and we were stuck in the old. **We used to take a lot of crap from these guys, but we had the last laugh**—because ultimately, **these nifty new high-tech ways of reaching people online became less and less effective.** Therefore, many of the gung-ho Internet marketing gurus, including the two who were in our organization, started teaching their clients about this really exciting way to drive traffic to your websites by using direct mail!

They returned to direct mail because they weren't getting the results they needed exclusively by selling online. Now sure, some people are still doing it all online; but I think you're seeing most Internet marketers come to the realization that adding direct mail to their Internet business is making them more profits than they were making exclusively online. **Even if you're an Internet marketer, you need to seriously consider the benefits of adding direct mail to your mix and moving your prospects offline, so you can do more business with them that way.** They'll be more loyal to you, and they'll probably spend more money with you. And even if you always give them the option to go online and buy, there's something about building that relationship with a customer by mail that's so much more profitable than doing it exclusively online.

Everybody thinks that direct mail is so old-fashioned, and it is — but it can be mixed with all kinds of high-tech marketing methods. Just because people were using this method 100 or 150 years ago doesn't mean that you can't combine it with all kinds of modern technology to reach people in a better way. It's still an effective way to drive traffic to your website and other kinds of high-tech types of technology that can be added with it to tell your full sales story. That's the common denominator here: to tell your complete sales story. **Answer all the objections; make a case for why whatever it is that you're selling is worth far, far more than the money you're asking for it in exchange.**

The second story I want to tell you about is about control, because again, **direct mail is all about control.** Recently, we used one of those online services to send out a press release to a bunch of online journalists and others. Chris Lakey and I, we're copywriters. We've been writing copy now for many years, and we work well together. Well, we wrote this kick-butt, killer news release... but they wouldn't let us run it the way we wanted. We had to make all these changes. We had to play by their rules. All these changes, in my opinion, just watered it down. They were unnecessary.

Now, if we would have just sent out that press release in a direct mail package, which we do plan on doing, we wouldn't have had to worry about all these rules and regulations and so forth. I hate rules and regulations. I know they're important in some ways, but I didn't become an entrepreneur to have a bunch of people telling me what I could and couldn't do. **I like control, and direct mail lets you have full control. You don't have anybody who tries to play games and hold power over you. With direct mail, *you* have the power.** It feels good.

Now, the third story I want to tell you about is just how simple it can be to make millions of dollars with direct mail. Our whole strategy for over 20 years now has been very, very simple. **To start with, we have something we call our new customer acquisition offer.** It's primarily direct mail. Throughout the years, we've done other kinds of advertising, but we've always come back to direct mail. That's been our mainstay.

This is a direct mail sales letter. It changes constantly, because we're always testing new things. We take the things that work the best, and they become part of our new customer acquisition control. **We have a direct mail package that goes out to the people that have never done business with us before, and it gets them to raise their hand or bite on an initial offer that we have that is either low-cost or, in some cases, even no-cost.** Our current new customer acquisition direct mail package asks for $9. Why $9? Because we tested several different prices, and $9 works best.

This is the first step in selling a $3,000 package, and a $9 front-end offer sells that most effectively. If we'd given it away for free, we wouldn't have been able to convert enough of the $3,000 sales to make a profit. When we charged larger amounts of money, fewer people responded. **Ultimately, ROI—return on investment—is that all that matters, and we got a better**

119

STEALTH MARKETING!

ROI with a $9 front end. For $9 we give them a hell of a deal, and they're very happy. They can't even believe what they got for $9! **So now they're in just the right frame of mind to take a serious look at what we want to sell them for $3,000.**

It's a very simple direct mail package. It contains a nice little booklet, and there's a personalized cover letter that shows through a double-window manila envelope. It looks official. It doesn't have anything phony on it to make it look like it's a government letter or anything like that, like you see some people do, but it's a very conservative-looking, plain brown envelope. They can see their name in one window, and a special offer in the upper window. The booklet is 20 pages long, with a nice full-color cover. Then there's an 8.5 x 14 order form that sells that $9 offer.

They get a nice, big package for their $9, by the way. **Then we try to upsell them on the $3,000 sale, so we do a whole bunch of follow up marketing with fliers, postcards, and letters, all of which try to upsell them.** That follow up marketing even includes live salespeople: if they have any questions, they can call one of our client service reps.

By that way, that's one of the greatest breakthroughs that has happened to our company in the last six or seven years. Drew Hanson, our Vice President of Client Relations, has put together an excellent sales force. These are honest salespeople with plenty of integrity, and boy, do they know how to sell! **That integrity is absolutely crucial, by the way.** The worst thing you can do is hire greedy salespeople who have no scruples, who end up telling the customer all kinds of lies, causing the customers to be unhappy so that they never buy from you again. Worse, they can get you into all kinds of legal troubles. **Our sales department is built on honesty and integrity.**

Using salespeople in conjunction with all these follow-up direct mail packages gives those packages even more power. **Having live salespeople always available if the customer has any issue is just one part of our effort to do everything possible to do a complete job of selling.** Now, that's just for new customer acquisition—the campaign that goes out there to attract new customers and that includes all the follow-up marketing and that upsell. **And then we have our bread and butter: our house list.** This includes all the people who have brought from us in the past, people that we already have relationships with. They know us, and they like us. There's trust that's been developed between us, because they've done business with us before, and they've always gotten much more than their money's worth. **That's why we go back to those people again and again, and make them offers that are similar to what they bought from us the first time.** That's it. That's our whole direct mail marketing plan.

And talk about control! We made a bold move about four months ago. For 20+ years we were using a mailing house to do all our inserting and mailings. It got to the point where we were paying them an average of $9,000 a week to do our direct mailing. **But now, we're doing all our own mailing house work.** I don't want you to think for one minute that this all just happened smoothly, okay? In fact, we're only about four months into this, and we still have problems to overcome. We haven't perfected it yet, but we're making progress. We still work with a partner in Wichita who does all of our bulk mailings, because of the technical difficulties in being able to send out such mailings; and anything over an ounce we pretty much send as bulk, as a general rule. **But we're essentially our own mailing house, so that's even more control that we're taking on.**

Again, I feel that it was a bold move on our part: we only did it after more than 20 years of being in the business. Quite frankly, we were looking for a way to cut some of our costs; but making the investment in all the necessary equipment and the operation in general was indicative of our total commitment for direct mail. Now Chris and I can get an idea on a Monday, and by Wednesday or Thursday we can put thousands of small offers in the mail to our customers. **It's almost as fast as email! But it's more effective than email—more expensive, sure, but more effective.**

Speaking of expense: in my opinion, people are usually too worried about the cost of everything. **You need to keep this in mind: cost** *only* **matters in relation to how much money it makes you.** All these Internet people are always all talking about the low cost of email, and they're right. But zero cost often means zero response. People just aren't responding to it, so who cares if it doesn't cost you any money? It's not making you any money, either. **The point is to develop a profitable system, and not angst over how much a piece of it costs.**

That's something that's just lost on a lot of people. You're not going to save money or profit on every little thing. **What you really need to think about is how your business brings in new customers, and then from that builds a relationship with them that turns into long-term profits.** That's why we have this little $9 front-end new customer acquisition offer, to funnel leads and prospects into our pool. **We have a back-end sale that's related to that that we hope as many people as possible will take, and when they do,** *that's* **when we earn our first profit.** And then, of course, we hope to do more business with them, selling them other products and services as well. That becomes the lifeblood of our business.

In relation to that, let's take a closer look at the value of testing. Most people want to develop ways for their businesses to work on autopilot, as we discussed earlier, and that's certainly possible. A good promotion can be that; in fact, our new customer acquisition model hasn't changed much in the last several months. In essence, it does run on autopilot. But during the time that we've used this model, we've consistently tested it to try to find ways to make it work better. Our main front-end offer is currently at $9, but it's been free, it's been $19, it's been $29, and it's even been $39. We've tested it thoroughly. The whole purpose of that offer is to get people to raise their hands and express interest in doing business with us. **That tells us that they're interested in the kinds of products and services we sell. We can then offer them additional products and services that are closely related to what they bought from us the first time.**

That's why we test different prices: to bring in the biggest number of the most qualified leads. If you have the price too low, you open the floodgates a little too much. You can bring in more prospects, but they don't respond as well on the back-end. So your conversion rates suffer, and you end up not making a profit, even though you brought in a bunch of leads. On the opposite end of the scale, when you set the initial price too high, you bring in a smaller number of leads that are more highly qualified. That's what happened when we raised the price of our new customer acquisition offer to $39. People responded at a better rate than the free leads, but there just weren't that many of them, and that wasn't profitable, either. We weren't able to convert those leads to sales, because we'd closed the floodgate too tight.

Once you have those parameters, you can start working on finding the happy medium. **That middle ground is where all your profits are made.** We found that $9 was a the sweet spot for us. It was a good qualifying amount; they had to put a little money into the game, but not too much. That raised the response rate to a level that we were satisfied with. **We brought in enough leads and then had a good enough conversion rate with those leads to make it profitable.**

So as you look at your direct mail campaigns, **look at both parts of the process.** The first part of lead generation is to bring in as many highly-qualified leads as possible; and then, on the backside of that, to be able to convert as many of those leads as possible to sales. **How you do that in tandem, how you get those two things clicking and working properly, will determine the success or failure of your business.**

Now, you have to continue doing business with your existing customers, the ones you have a relationship with, as long as possible; that's a cardinal rule of good marketing. But that will only sustain you so long. The pool will eventually dry up, as people's circumstances change, as they move, or as they pass away. **You need new customers coming in the door, so you have to go out and grab them.** The process of careful testing I've described here is how you do it. This is how we found out that the sweet spot on this offer was $9. In the past we've had other tests where we found out other things.

We test a lot, and the amount of testing we do depends on how confident we are in the offer we're running at that moment, and how new that offer is. But, for example, we've had periods of time in the past where we've been actively trying to do better with our front-end marketing, so we could bring in more customers. We've tested as many 10-12 different variants of offers or sales letters all at once. So if we've got a mailing list of 12,000 names, we might mail 1,000 of each of those 12 different pieces, analyzing the responses as they came back to us. Let's say three of those variants had horrible results. We'd throw those away immediately. Maybe four more were marginal; they made a little profit, but that was it. And then we might have four that worked fairly well, and one more that did a remarkably good job.

You look at that whole mailing test, and from that you decide which ones you want to retest, and you keep moving forward. So you're constantly testing; and once you have a control piece, once you *know* that something is working, the next step is to try to beat it. So you're constantly out there with new test pieces and test offers, trying to best what you're already doing, profit-wise.

This constant testing will lead you into all kinds of areas, because you're testing all kinds of different things. Sometimes we test things like envelope color; everything stays the same, except the envelope becomes green instead of yellow. Or maybe we'll try a different kind of envelope altogether, something with a different texture or text, or we'll try using a real stamp versus a metered one. We might try text that looks like real handwriting instead of laser-printing or typing. Beyond that, there are so many other things that you can test, including the color of the paper inside the envelope, the headlines, the price you're selling the item for—anything you can think of. **When you're truly testing, you're constantly in a state of motion with your offers, trying to find something that does better than what you're mailing right now.**

One of the things we're testing at the moment is what we call our Modified One-Step Offer. When I talk about marketing as a process of getting your leads to become costumers, **one of the things I talk about a lot is two-step marketing. That's where you get the leads to raise their hands first, then try to turn those leads into sales, into customers.** In some cases, it can take several weeks and even months before you see a payoff and make a profit. You've got all your expenses for your initial advertising; then you've got to deal with the response, the people who raise their hands and request more information. Then you've got the time and cost required to send those packages selling your main offer that you *hope* they will buy. Then you have to wait for those results to some back.

In the past, we've sometimes done a one-step offer, where you go straight for the sale. You don't ask them to raise their hand, and request more information from you or buy an introductory packet of some kind. In the example of our $9 offer where we generate leads, we would skip that step and just send them a sales package, trying to make the main sale. A certain percentage would buy, and the rest would not, and then we would be done. **The problem with that method is that you don't have a way to generate leads.** Either they buy or they don't buy, and what's done is done, and you move on to something else. What we're doing right now is modifying that one-step model; we're in the early phases of it, but we're pretty confident it will work, because we feel good about the offer. But we don't have the results yet, so I don't have any numbers to share.

In any case, here's what we're working on: **we're going to mail a one-step offer where we give them enough information that we feel like they could make a buying decision.** We hope that many of them will; but if they don't, **we're going to give them the option of going to our website, where they can read the full story.** In fact, we're backing up a shorter letter that goes for the sale with a longer, 32-page online sales letter in PDF format. So someone will be able to get our one-step offer in the mail and then, if they want to buy immediately, great: there's a form there, so they can make that purchase. **If they don't buy, if they're just interested, they can go on to our website and request more information about it, or even just read more information right online. They can even speak with one of our sales representatives if they have questions.**

That, we feel, could be the perfect combination that gets money coming in fast, because the benefits of a one-step offer is that you mail the offer out, and several days later you've got orders coming in. We're modifying the one-step model and allowing them to buy, or to go online and get more information, or call us and talk to us on the phone if they have questions. **We even give them an option of having a package mailed to them, if they choose that.** So we can build a list of people who got the offer but didn't buy right away, but we also have that immediate ability for them to instantly pay for the product, which hopefully puts us in the position to get into the profit faster. **We call that our Modified One-Step offer.**

And I'll throw out another thing here. Although we haven't widely used this method here at M.O.R.E., Inc., **I've seen other people make a low-priced lead generation offer, but include an option for the purchaser to check a box and go ahead and buy something else as well.** If enough people take advantage of this add-on, that helps you offset your cost of mailing—a significant consideration, since direct mail is notoriously expensive. So let's say you have a $9 main offer; you could easily add an option, maybe as a mention in a P.S., that they can get something more for a certain price, as long as they act right now. **Even if just a few of them take advantage of it, then you've made a little additional money to help offset the costs of your advertising and hopefully put you into profit that much faster.**

I want to re-emphasize here how valuable actually mailing someone can be in developing and maintaining a personal relationship. About two weeks ago, I sat down early one morning and I wrote my little sister a letter, put it in an envelope, and mailed it off to her. It took me about 20 minutes, and I didn't think much of it—although really, it's first time I've done that in years, because usually we just email back and forth with each other. Then I called her up last week and she thanked me for the letter, and she said, "Nobody ever sends me letters." That's so true. In this day and age, we're so inundated with technology that direct mail seems a bit old-fashioned. Yet when you do it right, it's loaded with sincerity, and it can be a very personal method of communication, not unlike the letter that I wrote to my sister. **It was a personal letter, and we should**

think of direct mail like that. In the end, it's all about relationships; direct mail lets you control even that.

And speaking of control: about two hours ago (as I write this), I sent Chris a link to the website of a woman in Denver who's selling a really cool business opportunity. But the price is right there in the headlines: $3,500. That just blew me away, because that's usually *not* what you want to lead with. With direct mail, you can have full control over everything. You can tell your whole story first; and then, once people get your whole story, they can see that the price you're asking for is very inexpensive. **You can chase people away by telling them too much, too fast**—like this lady in Denver has.

So stop calling it junk mail. It's not junk mail at all. Every time you get a direct mail package, even if it's coming from a major Fortune 500 company, think about why they've sent it. How do you think they became a major Fortune 500 company? They did it because they were in the right type of business in the right type of market, and they were doing the right kinds of things, including sending you that "junk mail" package. **So learn from these direct mail packages. Study them. Learn from watching other marketers.** Find what they're doing right and what they're doing wrong, as I did with this lady in Denver. Think about all the ways you can make things better still. Become a student of all this.

That's how it all starts for anyone who ultimately ends up making millions of dollars in marketing; **when you study their past, you see that it began with them having a deep interest in this kind of thing.** And direct mail is something you can get *very* interested in. **It's a highly creative form of marketing.** It's exciting. It's only limited by your imagination. You can always learn, and there is *so* much to learn here.

Earlier, I told you a bit about the Modified One-Step method we're testing right now. But there are so many different variations here, so many different things you can learn, that it's just amazing. **So I do want you to remember: school is never out for the pro. Keep your eyes open. Get on the other side of the cash register, and start speaking like a marketer and thinking like a businessperson.** Begin studying what other people are doing, and start developing that sense of what they're doing well or poorly. Look for the things that really excite you the most. Borrow and steal. And never stop testing!

Testing is a lot like fishing. Basically, you bait the hook, throw it out there, and wait for the bites. You never know exactly what you're going to reel in. You test a lot of different ideas, knowing that most of those tests are probably going to go nowhere. If you're testing to your best customers first, they're always going to show a little profit; **but your real winners are the items that your best customers are most excited about. Roll those out big.** That's how we develop our new customer acquisition promotions, you see: **we've internally done many stages of testing before we even begin to throw those offers out to people that have never done business with us before.**

This is something that, taken as a whole, can be worth literally millions of dollars to you. Or hundreds of thousands of dollars if that's all you want to make—or whatever your goals are. There are plenty of people who have learned how to do this. You can, too.

CHAPTER TEN

The power of take-away selling:

✓ <u>Nothing bothers people more than giving them something they really want</u> — <u>and then threatening to take it away</u>!

✓ The more they want it — and the more they <u>know</u> you can take it away — the more sales and profits you will make!

The Power of
Take-Away Selling

Nothing bothers people more than offering them something they really want... and then threatening to take it away. That's the basis of takeaway selling. **The more your prospect wants something, and the more they know that you can take it away, the more sales and profits you can make.**

Here's an example. We have an opportunity we're promoting right now, a contract we're offering our joint venture partners. They have to sign a seven-year agreement, and there's a major bonus they all want that's part of that opportunity. **But we're telling them that if they don't fulfill all of the obligations in that contract, the whole thing could become null and void.** In other words, they could lose something that they really want if they pull out. **By telling them that right up front, I promise you we're going to make a lot more money.** That one item in our agreement makes it clear that if they don't agree to all of these things, and they don't do certain things, then we're going to take away the thing they want the most. We're not hiding this in the least. These three lines of copy will make us more money, because they form a way for us to gain leverage in this deal.

That's what takeaway selling is. **It's all about power.** Now, power is just a perception, oftentimes; but he or she who controls that perception has the power.

Power is a funny thing. Let's look at the world of romantic relationships. During the ritual of dating, especially in the very beginning, if one person is too needy or appears to want the other person more, they have less power. That's an important point here: **whoever wants something more has *less* power, or at least the perception of less power. That's why part of this takeaway sales method is simply displaying that you're not desperate, because desperation is not an attractor.** Nobody wants to do business or associate with a desperate person. **It's the person who has confidence, the person who acts like they could take it or leave it, who's truly attractive.** Oh, they want your business; but they're not going to beg for it, because once you start to appear to be a little too desperate, you're weakened in the eyes of the other person.

That's why takeaway selling is largely about the perception of power. **It's also about supply and demand, and the perception that the supply is limited.** Again, think about the dating world, and some of the games that people play during dating rituals; and you'll see there's a little bit of takeaway selling involved there as well.

Here's a true story. Eileen and I got into some legal trouble after we'd been in business for less than three years. We'd never been involved in a situation like that before, and we were desperate; so we consulted this lawyer for help. We didn't know who he was, really, and he didn't know us. We sat down and we told him about our situation, and he wanted us to sign a contract immediately. There was a lot of money involved, and he wanted us to agree to pay him upfront. Eileen wanted to do it, and she was pressuring me to sign; but I didn't want to. I wanted to talk to other lawyers.

I was feeling a lot of resistance, but because I love my wife, I was getting ready to sign this piece of paper. And the lawyer just kept putting more and more pressure on us the whole time, trying to scare us into signing. And then, at one point, there was silence. He had the contract in front of us, and he was waiting for us to sign. He just shut up and we shut up, and everything was quiet for about five minutes. Then I noticed a bead of sweat on his forehead. I'm not being dramatic about this; this really did happen. A bead of sweat formed, and almost in slow motion, I saw it drip down his forehead. I saw that *he* was desperate! I saw behind the curtain for a minute, and realized that we were being manipulated. The man was literally sweating over us signing this contract. So I grabbed Eileen and we got the hell out of there.

Desperation is *not* an attractor. If you're desperate, the best thing you can do is pretend you're not. When you laugh, the world laughs with you. When you cry, you cry alone. That's as true in the marketing business as in any other part of life.

Here's a story that I love: there was a famous marketing expert who, in his early years, wasn't so famous. In fact, he was basically starving to death, because he had hardly any clients at all. But he didn't let his desperation show, ever, even though he badly needed work. If a prospective client happened to call him up about an initial consultation or about doing some small piece of work, the marketer would always say to them, "Hmmm... well, let me check my schedule so I can see what I have going on." And then he would pause... and there would be no schedule to check. There was nothing going on. The calendar was blank.

STEALTH MARKETING!

After letting the client wait for five minutes, he'd come back to the phone and say, "Next week is all booked up, and so is the week after that. But I can get you in three weeks from tomorrow. How does that sound?"

You can call that manipulation if you want. **That's fine, and it's acceptable if you're not hurting anyone by doing it.** It only becomes bad when you're trying to scam someone — when you're trying to sell them something that's worthless, or trying to get them to sign a contract when you know you can't deliver on your promises, or whatever. Otherwise, you're just stimulating their interest in working with you when you pull a stunt like that. **As soon as you've got something valuable — or something that** *appears* **valuable — people want to do business with you.** They want to be associated with other people who are movers and shakers, proven winners who are confident and have lots of bravado! **See, you have to give people what they want.** That's a basic tenet of business success. If that's what they want, that's who you have to be; and if you're not that, then you have to pretend that you are.

In marketing, the more the customer senses that you're desperate, that you desperately want something to work out, the more likely they are to run from that. **The more they sense that you're on top of the world, the more people want to get close to you so they can warm up next to your fire.** That's the way it's always been, that's the way it will always be, and why some people haven't figured it out yet is beyond me. And by the way, you've got to do things to create a real sense of urgency. Because everybody says, *Take action now! Limited time only!* Your prospects caught onto that long since. **The more you can** *honestly* **increase the perception that the supply is limited, the more you're going to increase the demand for it on the part of a good, qualified prospect.**

So, you've got to figure out how to work this perception of limited supply into your business message, along with the perception that while you'll welcome anyone's business, you're not desperately in need of it. If this is difficult for you, don't forget the Models concept. Look how other people are doing it; try to study that as much as you can, and then figure out how to get better at it yourself. This is something that may take you years to master, but the only way to get really good at it is by putting it into play and practicing the concept, tweaking and testing as you go.

The concept of takeaway selling is interesting in that it's a basic concept from non-business life that people can apply to their businesses. Many people, including entrepreneurs and other business owners, just miss the fact that **psychology is a large part of selling.** However, it makes sense when you really nail it down, because just about everyone understands the basics of economics—especially the simple nature of supply and demand. If supplies of something are high and demand is low, then the price becomes low. No one pays a lot of money for nails or oatmeal, because they don't have to. On the other side of the equation, **if you have something in extreme high demand and there's not very much of it, then you can command a high price for it, because the law of supply and demand dictates that you can.** When something is rare, the price people are willing to pay goes up accordingly.

Consider gold. As I'm writing this, the price has gone up

considerably over historic values, and the commodity is breaking all kinds of price records. It's bouncing between $1,300 and $1,400 per troy ounce. Demand is really strong right now, and there's only so much gold; the only way to make new gold is in a nuclear reactor, and that costs more than it's worth. So the law of supply and demand have caused the price of gold to skyrocket. Gold is a highly useful metal, and it's popular for jewelry; add in people's uncertainty over monetary policy and economics, and the price is rising rapidly.

Supply and demand is a force that most people understand—and yet for some reason, entrepreneurs often don't take advantage of it in selling situations. Well, it's the entire basis of takeaway selling. Takeaway selling is all about you taking power over the prospect by creating your product or service's level of supply and demand. **The actual supply may not be low, but if you establish the perception that it is, then you can drive the price up—and convince people to purchase it immediately instead of waiting.** Think about that marketing expert who didn't *really* have much on his books, but told people that it was going to be three weeks before they could get in to see him. He was creating a sense of demand in which the sparse commodity was his time.

If his time was wide open, if his schedule was clear and free, then that might have made a prospect wonder whether he was really that successful, and whether they should bother with them. How much is your time worth if your schedule is wide open? In order to create a demand, he made it appear that he was really busy; and the fact was, he could have been "really busy" playing golf or watching TV. But by creating the perception of limited time, he made the client believe that he was under high demand, which made his time very valuable—which naturally made him more attractive to the client. If I tell you I can only fit you in for 15 minutes and it's going to be three weeks before I can see you, my time becomes much more valuable than if I say, "Well, I've got nothing on my schedule, so you name the time and the place and I'll be there. Oh, and I can give you as much time as you want."

If you come across as desperate, then prospects feel like they're in control. If they know that you absolutely have to get this deal done, they'll ask for a better deal, and either lower the price they're willing to pay or ask for more (or both). On the other hand, **if they're under the impression that they're lucky just to be in a position to possible make a purchase, and they're at the risk of losing out if they don't, then their bargaining power is greatly reduced.** That's a situation where the seller holds all the cards.

Memorize and internalize this fact: *Supply and demand, or at least the perception of it, controls the price that someone is willing to pay for a product or service.*

That being the case, takeaway selling becomes the art of creating an environment in which you can maximize the value of your product or your service or your time. **Study your prospects and their psychology, and find ways to use takeaway selling.** Look at selling as a scale of seesaw; in any situation, you've got the balance of power tipping either toward you, or toward the prospect. You want those scales to be tipped in your favor as much as possible, and takeaway selling tips the balance in your favor.

139

STEALTH MARKETING!

Limited edition sets always become more valuable than unlimited edition sets, for example. You could go to any store and pick up a widget... but a widget hand signed by the artist who created it is in limited supply. There are only X number of these, and if you don't get one, you're going to have to make do with the regular one. So, if a standard widget costs $20, one of the hundred or so that's hand numbered and signed by the original inventor of the widget might fetch $200. It's no big deal if you don't care about it being signed; you can just go get a regular one off the shelf at the store. But if you're a collector, then you might be interested in these. The demand for the Limited Edition nature of it makes it cost more, and drives demand.

Over the weekend, Chris Lakey bought tickets to a basketball game that's happening six weeks from now. Tickets went on sale at 10:00 a.m. on Friday morning, and he knew that they only had so many tickets available. He knew that if he didn't buy when he could, he wasn't going to be able to see this game, which is being held at a different location than all the other games for this team. It was important to him to get tickets, so he knew that whatever it took, he needed to do it.

There were only few thousand seats to choose from, and Chris wanted the best available, so he made it a goal to be online at 10:00 to be able to snag the best seats he could. If he'd known that there were going to be 10,000 tickets available, and that the demand wasn't going to be very strong and he didn't think that it would sell out, he might have waited six more weeks to just walk up and buy tickets on the day of the game. However, he was afraid that demand would dictate that it *would* sell out quickly, that he wouldn't be able to wait and get a ticket later. So he needed to act as fast as possible to make sure that he got a good seat for this particular game.

It's the same way with any event where there's a limited number of something available. **If you feel like you risk losing out, you're much more willing to pay a higher price, and you're much less willing to negotiate. That's some of what takeaway selling gives you.** In whatever you're selling, you have to find that angle you can use to capitalize on this concept—whether it's a limited number of items, or it's available for a limited time. **Do what you can to make sure they know that you're *not* really desperate for their order, though you'll happily sell something to them.** Give them the impression you don't depend on them for your livelihood. While it may seem rude, some people actually say this outright in their copy. They don't worry about offending the prospect; they just tell them one way or another, "If you decide not to order today, I'll be okay with that. I have 30 other people waiting who *do* want to buy, so make the decision now or don't. If you say no, I'll just sell it to someone else. I don't need your order."

Now, the truth is always better than a lie, and usually will sell better anyway. **But within that framework, find an angle, a story that can limit the availability of your offer.** This is the heart of takeaway selling, and if you'll use this method you not only get more sales, you'll probably increase your average ticket price. That is, your average dollar amount per sale will go up, even as you find it easier to make sales.

But you've got to be willing to lose some sales to get there. If your offer's strong, don't be afraid to pass on a sale and make people sweat it out. **If you've got people fighting to order**

141

whatever it is, you'll always be in a better position to make profit. If you find a way to use takeaway selling, your business will soar. You'll have more sales, more profits, and your customers will be happier, because everybody wants to know they got a good deal. **Everybody wants to know they got something that wasn't just readily available.** You always feel best when you come home from the store and you've got that one find that maybe you shouldn't have gotten. Think about when you win an auction, that feeling you get when you were the highest bidder. Everybody wants to know that they got the good deal, that they got the prized possession that wasn't available to just anybody. And so your customers feel better, too. **All the way around, takeaway selling is something you definitely need to incorporate into your business.**

If you're not sure how to do this, just start paying attention to how other people do it. Here's an example. Think about some of the Internet marketers who tell you about all the money they're making and how successful they are. I happen to know the inside truth: A lot of those guys aren't nearly as successful as they want you to believe. Part of their power comes from them creating this illusion that they're hugely successful. **Again, perception is reality, and you have to learn how to control the perception to a degree. I'm not talking about lying to people; this is all about giving people what they want... and nobody wants to do business with someone they perceive as weak.**

CHAPTER ELEVEN

Great marketers *see opportunities* where others cannot.

Great Marketers See Opportunities Where Other People Cannot.

One of the definitions of a genius is someone who looks at the same situation that everybody else is looking at, but they see things entirely differently. Maybe they see possibilities where other people don't. Maybe they just see opportunities. They may see multiple ways of handling a situation where others only see one. In fact, I think that a genius is someone who can see many different things that aren't apparent to others.

I also believe that with a few exceptions, we all have it within us to be much more creative, much more like what some people would call a genius. But this is something you have to work at, especially when you're in the marketing business. It's all about dreaming up ideas for a product, services, and opportunities that will sell well in your marketplace; **and in order to do that, you have to start with the market.** You can't really start with the idea and then figure out who you're going to sell it to. What's important is the customer, the person you're trying to do business with. What do they want more than anything else?

And you really do have to think that through in a deep, careful way, so that you can come up with the best answers. That takes time and work. You have to think, and I suggest that you do so on paper, where you can more easily sketch all of this out.

STEALTH MARKETING!

Who are these people you're trying to sell to?

Your job is to know your market in an intimate way.
After some deep thought, you'll start getting some clues as to what they really want, both in terms of what they've bought from you in the past and what they're buying from other people. **Once you've studied several hundred effective sales letters or websites that other people are using to reach this opportunity market, you'll begin to see common denominators.** Things will become visible that were invisible before. You'll start to see patterns emerge. **That's how you start developing an innate awareness of what it is that people really want: when you start seeing the same benefits over and over again in the same types of offers.** This may take years... and I don't say that to discourage you. The point is, you have the ability here to make incredible amounts of money if you get it right, so all this effort is worth it.

Think about college. Most people go to college for four to six years, and they struggle a lot. They have to pay a tremendous price in terms of money and effort in order to get that degree; but in the end, it's worth it. Same here. Once you start developing concrete ideas about what your prospects want, then you can start going to the next phase—which is another question, one that you have to keep asking all the time, so often that it eventually becomes part of your subconscious. And that question is: **How can I give it to them bigger, faster, and easier in a more effective way?** How can I serve up more of what I *know* that they want the most, better than anybody else? When you live with these questions long enough, the answers will come—answers that wouldn't have if you hadn't put some deep thought into the matter

If you're looking for an easier way to get there, I don't know of one. It takes a lot of effort to develop this marketing genius ability, this creative power that lets you see things that other people can't. **But once you do, you can create so many things that make that cash register ring. And as you do so, you can't get hung up on details.**

I had the great privilege of spending some time with one of our joint venture partners and friends this past weekend. And as I took him to the airport yesterday, we had a little time to kill, so we were talking and trying to sum up some of the ideas that we're working on together and want to proceed with. I asked for a bit of clarification on the two offers he's making money with right now, and for one of the offers, he said, "Well, it's kind of complicated." But when he told me what it was, I said, "That's not complicated!" He said that he'd had to explain it to his business partner again and again, and his partner still didn't quite understand it. Well, his business partner is a smart guy... but he's very analytical and detail-oriented.

If you're going to wake up that creative genius within you, you have to think in concepts, not details. Often, you need to start developing things before you have all the answers figured out. You just start working with ideas, almost in the way an artist would with a canvas or a mound of clay. That's the kind of relationship you need to have with ideas, so you're just trying all these different ideas on for size and playing with them to see if they work. It's not work in a traditional way, perhaps. **I see it as much more of an artistic, creative process.**

STEALTH MARKETING!

This morning was a good example. It's Monday now, and Chris Lakey and I hadn't spoken with each other for a few days. So this morning we got on the phone and started talking about a project we discussed last Thursday. I'd had time to think it through a bit, and so had he. We're deeply committed to trying to generate revenue for one of our companies that's behind this idea, so we just started playing with all these different ideas. We didn't have it all figured out, but we just started going back and forth. And then we've got a third business partner whom we brought into the whole thing; and things got a little frustrating there for a while... for me, anyway. There was a little push and pull from our business partner, and things just got a little frustrating and confusing, and then boom! It all pieced together in the end. **But it probably took us about 45 minutes to an hour before things really started becoming clear.** I think we've got a killer idea now that we didn't have when I woke up this morning.

I had already been thinking about some of the pieces of that idea since last Thursday, and I know Chris had been as well. **It's an exciting process, this going back and forth as we exchange our ideas, almost like a game.** That doesn't mean it's always a lot of fun; when you watch your favorite sports team lose a big game, for example, there's nothing fun about that. It's a lot of effort: those guys are out there hustling, getting bloody, breaking bones. Some of them are going to the hospital, so it's not necessarily a lot of fun... and yet it *is* a game, in the sense that it's not traditional work. **And this is a game where only the vaguest ideas are needed in the beginning, and you can figure things out as you go.** You can play with these ideas, and you can strengthen the concept, and let the different elements take on life of their own. Ideas evolve, especially when you're working on a big project where you want to make a lot of money.

I imagine that's why you're reading this: because you want to make a lot of money. **Well, some of the ways you can do that is to take ideas that worked before and find a way to put a new spin on them.** We've got a promotion out there right now that's in its sixth generation since we first introduced it five years ago. The joke is that if we're still going strong five years from now, which we plan on, then we might be in the 12th or 13th version of it. It will look different on the surface, of course, and some of the ideas will have different names. We'll come up with new themes, new angles, but essentially it will be the same thing. *That's* **the way you keep creating a lot of new products and services.** You just keep finding ways to put new spins on your old stuff. That's part of what being a marketing genius is about.

Now, it takes a lot of work to be creative. I talked about brainstorming with Chris, and of course we also brainstorm with our management team and our joint venture partners. **No man is an island: you need other people to help you play with these ideas.** It takes time and work... even if that work doesn't always look like work. Some mornings I just sit in the shower for a long time and think, coming up with ideas and writing them down. I'm trying to spark connections, intermixing ideas, hoping they'll cross-pollinate to create new ideas that lead to profitability.

Those are the ingredients that will ultimately lead to developing the next big thing. **So sweat it out, think deeply, brainstorm with other people, brainstorm with yourself, and write things out.** There will be a lot of chaff in with the wheat, but some of those ideas will be magical. I wish I could tell you that there's an easier, softer way, but I don't know of any. **You just have to think, think, think, and try to see the world from new and different angles that weren't obvious to you before.**

I think a lot of the greatest marketers are visionaries. They see things that other people overlook, or somehow aren't in tune to. Again, a lot of that comes from knowing your customers intimately—from putting yourself in their shoes and visualizing what it's like to be them, so you can develop the ability to see the kinds of offers they would be interested in responding to. Now, a good entrepreneur has the capacity to run in hundreds of different directions and do numerous things, and yet the ones who are the most successful stay focused on one area, or on a specific group of customers, or a marketplace that they're trying to dominate. **They come up with as many ways as possible to serve that marketplace, and make a profit by doing so.** Again, it starts with a marketplace; from there it evolves into a total commitment to serving that marketplace. This helps you see all the different ways of making your dream a reality.

One of the people who comes to mind in this regard is Richard Branson, the man who started Virgin Mobile, Virgin Records, and many other successful businesses. One reason he comes to mind is because he's had a mission to build a commercial spaceship for a while now, and that's something he's spent a fortune of his own money developing—feeling, I'm sure, that he could commercialize it and make a profit leveraging it as a business. Or consider Steven Fossett, Branson's rival and sometime ally. He was the first person to fly around the world in a balloon. Ultimately, he died in an airplane in the Nevada desert. But Fossett was always looking for that next adventure, and he spent a lifetime pursuing his passion of flying and of trying to accomplish feats that no one had ever accomplished before. I think he and Richard Branson saw opportunities out there to do things that they wanted to do. Some of what they did was personal, based on hobbies and passions; some was more broadly business based.

Business certainly involves the same kinds of aspirations. **It takes being completely dedicated to the business, and to the task of becoming as great as you can be in your marketplace**—becoming the kind of entrepreneur people write books about. When you're in that mode, when you've become that person, you see things in a different light. They say that the great hitters in baseball are like that. They're so focused on the ball that they see it coming every inch of the way, no matter how fast the pitcher hurls it. They have such great concentration and vision that they can pick out every detail, including the rotation, which tells whether it's a curve or a slider or a fast ball or a knuckle ball, and they can adapt to that on the fly.

That kind of concentration on the mission, that determination and focus, plays a big part in any entrepreneur's ability to truly see the marketplace in front of them and react to it, doing things that other people can't. Those other people simply don't have that dedication and concentration, so it seems like magic to them when the marketing geniuses adapt to the marketplace without batting an eye. But it's just a matter of being able to read the nuances; that's how a great marketer manages to see those opportunities that others cannot. **It's a total dedication to your craft, a**

matter of totally being in tune to your marketplace. That's what separates those who just play around at being an entrepreneur from the serious people who end up making millions of dollars.

Those who have this kind of vision are the ones who dominate, and don't fool yourself into thinking that it comes naturally or that these people are special. **It all boils down to commitment and dedication.** As with everything else, you get out of it what you put into it. Everybody wants all the great results, but few of us want to keep putting in the necessary time, work, effort, and energy. The few that do are the ones who stand out. **Simply put, great marketers aren't born great; All the things that I'm talking about here are skills that can be developed.** Even creativity is a skill. People don't think of it as such, but it truly is. Are some people more apt to be creative? Of course they are. But don't use that as an excuse for not putting in the necessary time and work and effort.

And here's a little secret: the more you enjoy something, the less work it is. So fall in love with marketing. It's a lot of fun. It's challenging and frustrating at times, and it's not always easy. And yet, all the greatest things, the things we get the most joy from, tend to fall into the category of things that you have to pay a high price for.

CHAPTER TWELVE

If you <u>only</u> knew just how apathetic people are when they read your sales material you'd be shocked!

➤ There are exceptions — but most people don't care! They have a great deal of unconscious (or even conscious) resistance <u>against</u> what you are saying.

➤ You <u>must</u> be totally aware of this — <u>before</u> you can develop the correct strategies to deal with it.

Overcome the Apathy

If you only knew just how apathetic people are when they're subjected to your sales material, you would be absolutely shocked! There are some exceptions, of course, but the fact is that most people just don't care. **Most have a great deal of unconscious or conscious resistance to what you're telling them. You've got to be totally aware of this before you can develop the correct strategies to deal with it.**

I've got a friend who recently sent me an email link to something new that he's doing, and he's all excited about it. He goes, "You're going to love this, TJ!" Well, I couldn't make the link work, so I don't know yet; but maybe so, maybe not. I'm involved in so many other things that chances are, I'm *not* going to love it like he loves it.

But that's okay. In order to do a good job of selling whatever it is that you're selling, you have to be totally passionate about it. **You have to believe in it deeply. You have to be 100% sold before you can sell.** The danger is to think that just because *you're* in that frame of mind, other people will be, too. They're probably not. **It's up to you to try to transfer your emotions to them; that's one of the definitions of what selling is all about.** You're in love with what you're selling. You make *them* in love with it. But that process—and it *is* a process—takes time and strategy and money. Throughout that process, you have to realize just how apathetic people are, how skeptical they are, how lazy they are, how resistant to your sales message they are, how *jaded* they are.

Most listeners don't believe a damned word you say; and even if some of them do, you have to assume that they don't. Now, some people might say, "Oh man, that's negative!" Yeah, it is—but you achieve a positive goal here by starting with the negative assumption. If you assume everyone is apathetic and skeptical, or at least somewhat jaded and cynical, then **it's up to you to prove to them that what you have is worthy of their love.** And so many people just don't get it! Selling is a *process*, involving multiple steps. You can't just do a little and expect a lot in return. If you want a big, huge result, it takes a lot of work to get that. **If you want somebody to spend a lot of money with you, you're going to really have to put something great together.**

Just to give you an example: we've got a new offer we're playing with right now, one we're getting ready to test to our customers. It's going to be a fairly low-cost offer; we're going to be testing different price points, some as low as $149 or so, but we know it will be well under $400. What we're offering is huge for such a low price. We're not going to go out and do a whole lot of follow-up marketing, so we need to get them the first time. We're not doing this in a two-step fashion, either; we're trying to get it sold right away. So, we're putting this huge offer together where they get thousands of dollars worth of valuable information products that have been prepared in a special technology so they're digitally delivered. This allows us to keep our costs super-low. Now, the fact that we're making them this unbelievable offer for a small amount of money might get some attention—but it's also going to cause their skepticism to skyrocket.

To overcome that skepticism, we're giving them so many details it's not even funny. **If they want to take the time, we're going to have a 40-50 page document online that will show them in extremely detailed language exactly what we're giving them for such a low price.** We don't expect people to read it word-for-word, but we do want them to scroll through it all, so that they can prove to themselves that this is real. We're going overboard here, and thank goodness we're able to use the Internet to help us deliver those sales messages! If you had to print it out and send 40-50 pages to people, it would be expensive. **But we'll use a small sales letter to get people to go to the website, and the website will do the bigger selling job.**

The point I want to make is, we're not just *telling* **them it's a great thing. We'll have a preponderance of proof.** We're going overboard—and you have to go overboard! People don't believe a damned word you say, so you'd better prove it. In this case, we're offering them the Master Joint Ownership License to about 150 products, and we're going to be so specific in the details about what all these products are, and what their real value is, that anybody that goes through it is going to be totally overwhelmed. **So we're overcoming all of that resistance,** all of what some people would call the negatives—the fact that people don't believe anything, that they're skeptical.

You also have to realize that they're trying hard to hold onto their money, too. They only have a limited amount of cash, and there's only so much room left on their credit cards. A lot of these people are strapped already. You're not the only one pitching to them. Take that into account. You'll see why you'll need to go overboard.

We've got another brand new offer out there, and the sales letter is 47 pages long. The price point on that one is going to be just under $500. You might say, "What kind of person reads a 47-page sales letter?" The truth is, hardly anybody; **but they *do* scan them.** And if you're trying to tell people you've got an unbelievable deal they might be attracted to, well, people are attracted to hype; there's no question about it. But you'd better do something to support that hype, because of how doubtful people are. You'd better go overboard, because they're resistant to giving you their money. **The more they know, the more you can effectively deal with them.** So don't be afraid to go overboard.

I think that in a perfect world, things would be very simple. You'd just say, "This is what I'm selling. This is how much I'm selling it for. Here's how you get it." You could write it on a single note card, and everybody who was in your marketplace would read it. They'd quickly see what you were offering. Some of them would be interested. They would buy, and everybody would go home happy.

That's not the way it works.

People are apathetic and busy, and don't really care whether your business is there or not. Now, let's say you have a fast food restaurant. Well, everybody has to eat, but they're still apathetic, and they still don't really care that you're there. They know that if you *weren't* there, somebody else would be. So accept that in all marketplaces, people really don't care about your business *per se.* **They care about what is self-serving to them. They care about their own lives, not yours.**

Most people are worried about making their car payment or their house note, or about buying groceries. They care about what's right in front of them, making sure that their family's taken care of first. Not that these are all selfish things, necessarily, but they're all self-serving. People really don't think much beyond their own four walls, so they certainly aren't intent on doing business with you just because you exist and have a product. **If you start out with this assumption, it allows you to think more about how to craft your offers so that you can make it self-serving for them, which will make them more likely to respond.**

How can you make it so that they want to do business with you because of what they're going to get out of the transaction? That's the question you need to ask yourself. So before you start to develop the marketing strategy you're going to use to sell to them, you've got to remember that with very few exceptions, the people in your chosen marketplace really just don't care about you, your business, your product or your service. Accept that. Learn to live with it. **They could take or leave you, but hopefully they'll want a benefit that you're offering. That apathy should drive your angle. It should drive your hook. It should be what's making you craft your offer in such a way that, hopefully, you get the biggest response.**

Many people don't really even realize that they have this built-in selfishness. If you ask a hundred people, "Are you a selfish person?", most will say, "No." And yet their buying habits, their spending habits, their lifestyles, their behaviors all dictate otherwise. They live in a bubble for the most part, and they take care of Number One; and maybe if they have a family, they're concerned about their family's affairs, but they really don't think much beyond that. They couldn't tell you that they're concerned mostly about their own self; that's just the way they behave. So you're not going to get a survey out of them, at least not as such.

It would be so great if we could just mail a survey to our customers and ask, "What kind of things do you want to buy? Because we would love to give you exactly what you want. It's our goal to serve you, and we want to give you whatever it is that you want the most." If we did that, though, it would be futile. We'd get back some answers, sure; some people would tell us things, but most don't really know. **You discover these things by studying your marketplace, by repeatedly going back to an intimate knowledge of who your customers are and what kinds of things they're already buying.**

You have to enter into the conversation that they're already having in their heads. That's a phrase you've seen me use before, and I'm repeating it because it's critical. By knowing your prospects and customers intimately, you can start to get a feeling for the things that they're selfish about, the things that are important to them. It's your goal as an entrepreneur to figure these things out, because you already know that they're apathetic, right? You know that they don't care about you *per se*. **They're only concerned about what's right in front of them, so you have to figure out what those things are, and then sell to them in such a way that conveys the message that what you have is important to them.** Not important because you *said* it was important, but because their buying behavior has told you that it's important to them.

You have to break through the apathy by spending time getting to know who your prospects are, and then by finding ways to give them what their selfishness already makes them want. Answer that question, "What do they really want the most?", and you'll be able to break through that apathy and get them to want to pay attention to you. **The only way you're going to make sales is to get them to pay attention, and the only way they're going to pay attention is if you serve their selfish interests.** If you can solve that equation, they'll play right into your hands, and you'll play right into theirs. **They want to know "What's in it for me?" You grab their attention by firmly answering that question.**

Reselling to the same basic customers over and over again is the real secret to maximum profitability. You shouldn't always be out there chasing new customers; you need to maximize your existing customer base. We're all kind of like politicians, in that in order to get re-elected, we have to keep our constituents happy. **We have to keep making big promises and then fulfilling on those promises.** There's some selfishness involved on both sides of the equation. A lot of people don't like to admit that they're selfish. They would like to think they're above it, but that's not reality. When it comes to spending money, people are extremely selfish! **There are some exceptions, but for the most part, people buy only for a small number of reasons: greed, fear, and pride.** There's often a selfish, self-serving reason why they buy and what they're looking for. They buy to feel good about themselves. **The psychology of that changes from market to market, but it's locked into powerful emotions that are based on self-centeredness.**

Somehow, some way, they're trying to feel better about themselves. Some marketers base their whole approach around this tenet, because the truth of it is self-evident for anyone willing to look. There are probably other reasons that are equally as important, but I think it really does all come down to selfishness at some level. **People buy for their own selfish, self-centered reasons. You don't have to like that, but you do have to accept it if you want to be a good marketer and make a lot of money.** So what I would suggest to you is that in order to really understand this, start trying to get inside your own heart and head.

All people buy unconsciously for the most part: me, you, and all your prospects. Often, the purchases are based on emotion. Knowing that, the more you can try to analyze yourself, and figure out why you do what you do, the more you'll understand the motivations of others—especially if you're selling to people who buy the same kinds of things that you buy. That's when this exercise really becomes apropos. So sit down and think about it... figure these basics out, and just try to realize that nobody's ever going to love your stuff as much as you do. Sorry, but it's true!

Nobody, ever, is going to feel the way that you feel about your products and services, whatever it is that you sell. **You're making a big, *big* mistake if you don't start with the assumption that they really don't care.** No matter how much they might try to pretend they do, you have to assume that they don't. **If you do that, if you start with the premise that you really have to win people over every single time, then you'll make a lot more money in the end.**

CHAPTER THIRTEEN

✳ ✳ ✳

The adversities in life can make us stronger... and that's great, because business is a constant adversity.

✳ ✳ ✳

Adversity Can
Make Us Stronger

The adversities we face in life can make us stronger, and that's a great thing—because business is constant adversity. That's how it seems to me, anyway, and I believe that most other entrepreneurs would say the same.

You know, a lot of people start businesses because they want a better life. The truth is, life (as I know it anyway) is just a constant series of problems, challenges, obstacles, setbacks, disappointments, and suffering at various levels. **And business is life amplified. Now, I'm not saying that life is terrible; it's also full of good stuff, too. You get plenty of that good stuff in business; in fact, generally, you get more of the good than the bad.** But you *do* get plenty of the bad stuff.

While it's true that adversity can break some people, the same adversity can cause other people to break records. There's a quote from Nietzsche that I love: "Whatever doesn't kill you makes you stronger." **In large part, the difficulties we face in life help us develop our skills and abilities, which inevitably makes us stronger.**

In most cases, what matters is what you choose to do with the situation you find yourself in. As another of my favorite quotes points out, **"Adversity introduces you to yourself."** You really find out what you're made of when you have to deal with 10 tons of crap at once. **By taking on more,**

not less, you find out what you're truly capable of. Now, sometimes you do have moments when you break down or have trouble moving forward. **But remember: skills are developed through adversity.** During the smooth times, when everything comes easily, when you're not struggling, when you don't have to pay a large price, you don't really learn anything. You don't develop special abilities and talents.

That's the way most people want to live: they want to move through life unscathed, like they're floating on a gentle, peaceful river. And who can blame them? Who in their right mind *really* wants a life that's filled with all kinds of adversity and challenges? **But when you study the lives of the most successful people, you'll find a common denominator running like a golden thread through their stories: they went through *more* problems than other people, not fewer.** They faced more challenges and struggle than most, and that's part of how they acquired that level of mastery that enabled them to achieve the level of significance that ensures that they actually have a biography that's worth studying.

Again, I'm speaking in generalities here: **but whether you're broken by adversity, or push through it to break records, is based primarily on the way that you look at the problems, obstacles, and setbacks you face.** You can either look at them in a good, positive way, and decide that they're not going to beat you, and keep moving forward—or you can back off.

Back in 1985, when I first decided to go into business for myself, I told a good friend of mine. She was much smarter than me, had much more common sense than I probably still have, and she really cared about me... and so she did everything she could to discourage me. She was unsuccessful, so she went and got another friend of ours, and he started pounding on me too. All their arguments were just so rational: they were just trying to remind me that I had *none* of the qualities that it takes to succeed in business.

And they were right. I *had* none of those qualities then; and 25 years later, in many cases, I still don't. **But I *have* learned to delegate, and I've surrounded myself with people who possess those qualities that I lack. Plus, I was willing to do whatever it took to succeed... and it did require a tremendous price.** I had *no idea* that it was going to take the kind of price that I've had to pay. I'm not complaining or whining; I really don't think that's a bad thing, in any sense. But the fact is that back then, I had absolutely no clue what I was going to have to go through in order to get where I am today... and I probably still have a lot more to go through beyond this. I have no idea, thank God. There's bit of a blessing in being ignorant. I heard, somewhere along the line, that you've got to be a little bit stupid to think you can go out there and make millions of dollars.

I've known a gentleman for 20 years who's a Mensa member—and you have to have an IQ off the charts just to become one. He's got entrepreneurial qualities, and for years I've told him, "Look, you ought to be self-employed. You ought to be an entrepreneur." He's got the desire to do it... but he keeps saying that he knows too many ways that a business can fail. He studied business in college, so he knows about all the things that can go wrong. **Whereas somebody else who lacks that awareness, somebody who's more ignorant than he is, is**

more likely to charge ahead and plow through it, and just figure out a way to make it work.

Skills are developed through adversity—through encountering all the problems and the pain and the setbacks, and trying to make the best of it, trying to salvage some good out of it, trying to turn lemons into lemonade—trying to just not let it defeat you. And it does make you stronger.

Back in 1987, I told my Dad that I was going to get married, and to my face he was supportive. But there are no secrets in my family; everybody loves to gossip. To my sister Carla, my Dad said, "T.J. just isn't ready for marriage." Of course, then she told me, and I got all pissed about it. But you know what? He was right; I *wasn't* ready for marriage. I wasn't ready for business, either. I wasn't ready to take on any of those responsibilities, but the thing is, I would never have been ready for any of it. **There would never have come a perfect time for me to start a business *or* get married—but my marriage and my business are two of the things that give me the greatest satisfaction in life today.** By most people's standards, I would never have been ready; I lacked all of the right qualities, and in some ways I still do—ask my wife! **I still have a long way to go, but I've gotten to where I am by dealing with what I had to deal with and going through it.** That's the way people become strong. That's how they develop.

All of these things have to be developed; that's just reality. But no one likes to talk about adversity. No one likes to admit we're suffering from it. And yet, we all experience it, and it really *can* make you stronger—if we're willing to use it and learn from it. I think the word "can" is important in this principle. **The**

adversities in life *can* **make us stronger; and that's great, because business is a constant adversity.** I think the opportunity exists for adversity to grow you, if you will; though unfortunately for some people, I think adversity makes them break down. **I think that adversity can wilt a person.** Some people can succumb to it... so ultimately, the opportunity is there for it to have either effect.

How you handle those adversities will determine if it's a growing experience for you. **Martin Luther King, Jr. once said, "The ultimate measure of a man is not where he stands in moments of comfort and convenience, but where he stands at times of challenge and controversy."** So think about that. This could apply to you in any part of your life, business or personally. Your ultimate measure in life or in business is in how you handle and respond to challenges, controversies, inconveniences, and things that don't go your way. It's easy to pretend that life's great when things are going well; it's a lot harder to keep your chin up when you're up against the wall.

When business is going well, money's flowing easily and things are about as good as they could be. Everybody is happy. There are no problems to speak of. In those moments, it's easy to put on a happy face. It's easy to say that everything is going great and that you're doing well, isn't it? Then, when business becomes hard, when things aren't going well, that same person who was so happy when business was good is suddenly crabby to be around. They've always got a frown on their face, or they're always mad. **They're a product of their circumstances, no matter what the circumstances are.** When things are well, they're okay. When things aren't well, they're not so okay.

That's why the measure of a person is more in how they respond to adversity than how they respond when things are going well. I think that's the point here: **you can be made stronger by adversity, but you have to treat it the right way.** In business, there are always going to be challenges. Even when you have a successful business, there are going to be tough times. Sometimes, successful businesses seem to have big targets on their backs *because* they're successful. **People don't necessarily take to success like you would think they would; some are jealous of it.** If you have a big successful business, your competitors might want to sue you. They might want to talk bad about you in public, or say bad things on the Internet about your company because they don't like you. They think you're too successful. They think you're too big. And of course, if you're big and successful, the government wants a piece of that through a bigger tax percentage, or you may be more prone to get audited by the IRS.

There are all kinds of things that come with success, and then, obviously, on the flip side of that, there are all kinds of problems that occur when things aren't going well and business is suffering. **How you handle those adversities, how you handle the ups and downs, the challenges of business, will determine your ultimate character.** Those things have the opportunities to grow you and make you stronger, but you've got to survive them first. You can't succumb to them.

I'll be the first to admit that business can be frustrating and challenging, especially when you're building a new business. The ultimate success rate for new businesses is about 5%; that is, approximately 95% of businesses don't make it to their fifth anniversary. Even among the 5% that do, some just barely make it. Many of those businesses face a ton of things that don't go right during that initial start-up and growth phase. **Well, the ability of those business owners to see it through those times when things are ugly has a lot to do with whether they make it to that five year mark or not.** When things aren't going well, you really do learn a lot more about your mettle, and your ability and desire to stick it out.

Adversities can make you stronger, if you'll let them—and if you'll work through them and use them as a springboard to future success. So adversity isn't a foreign concept; we all deal with it. **How you respond to it will determine, ultimately, your success or failure.** If you study the biographies of successful people, you'll see a pattern of them going through some very difficult periods; and yet they got through it all, and in the end things worked out for them. The same thing can happen to you, too.

And just as adversity introduces you to yourself, it also introduces you to the people around you. **The best way to find out about other people, and to find out what they're made of, is go through some difficulty with them.**

www.ingramcontent.com/pod-product-compliance
Lightning Source LLC
Chambersburg PA
CBHW020205200326
41521CB00005BA/251